"Dennis Rainey has hit another home run!"

"PULLING WEEDS, PLANTING SEEDS is a thought-provoking blend of God-given truths, memorable nostalgia, and homemade happiness...A more fruitful harvest awaits all who will take the time to read and heed these pages."

CYNTHIA SWINDOLL
Executive Vice President
Insight for Living

"...This book is not pious theory. Dennis writes from the workshop of reality and has produced an heirloom..."

HOWARD G. HENDRICKS
Chairman, Center for Christian Leadership
Dallas Theological Seminary

"...I highly recommend that you spend time working through the crucial issues of this fascinating book."

BRUCE H. WILKINSON
President and Founder
Walk Thru the Bible Ministries

"I stand firmly behind the work of Dennis Rainey and the Family Ministry and most certainly encourage the reading of PULLING WEEDS, PLANTING SEEDS."

TOM LANDRY
Dallas Cowboys

"With wholehearted endorsement, I would like to recommend Dennis Rainey's book, PULLING WEEDS, PLANTING SEEDS. It is filled with common sense and wisdom..."

FRANK MINIRTH, M.D.
Minirth-Meier Clinic

"Dennis Rainey is a creative and talented writer but, even more important, he is a dedicated husband and father. [He] speaks and writes the language of everyday life..."

BILL BRIGHT
President and Founder
Campus Crusade for Christ

"...PULLING WEEDS, PLANTING SEEDS is proof positive that this author has a brilliant mind, a loving father's heart, and a world-class pen."

BOBB BIEHL
President
Master Planning Group International

Pulling Weeds, Planting Seeds

DENNIS RAINEY

Here's Life Publishers

First Printing, February 1989

Published by
HERE'S LIFE PUBLISHERS, INC.
P. O. Box 1576
San Bernardino, CA 92402

Library of Congress Cataloging-in-Publication Data
Rainey, Dennis, 1948-
   Pulling weeds, planting seeds : growing character in your life and
family / Dennis Rainey.
   p.   cm.
   ISBN 0-89840-217-4
   1. Christian life—1960- .   2. Family—Religious life.   I. Title.
BV4501.2.R32   1988
248.4—dc 19   88-39355
                    CIP

Scripture quotations designated NIV are from *The Holy Bible, New International Version,* © 1978 by the New York International Bible Society, published by the Zondervan Corporation, Grand Rapids, Michigan.

Scripture quotations designated TLB are from *The Living Bible,* © 1971 by Tyndale House Publishers, Wheaton, Illinois.

Scripture quotations designated NASB are from *The New American Standard Bible,* © The Lockman Foundation 1960, 1962, 1963, 1968, 1971, 1972, 1975, 1977.

For More Information, Write:
L.I.F.E.—P.O. Box A399, Sydney South 2000, Australia
Campus Crusade for Christ of Canada—Box 300, Vancouver, B.C., V6C 2X3, Canada
Campus Crusade for Christ—Pearl Assurance House, 4 Temple Row, Birmingham, B2 5HG, England
Lay Institute for Evangelism—P.O. Box 8786, Auckland 3, New Zealand
Campus Crusade for Christ—P.O. Box 240, Colombo Court Post Office, Singapore 9117
Great Commission Movement of Nigeria—P.O. Box 500, Jos, Plateau State Nigeria, West Africa
Campus Crusade for Christ International—Arrowhead Springs, San Bernardino, CA 92414, U.S.A.

Dedicated to

Jeff Tikson

We think you're great!
All eight of us do!
Your servant spirit
and friendship
are appreciated.
We love you.

Acknowledgments

Sue Stinson and Jeff Schulte deserve a special medal of commendation for their patience and hard work on the numerous manuscript drafts and revisions. Sue, you are one incredible lady and a gracious person to put up with me and to serve our family so faithfully. Jeff, your diplomacy and juggling ability continues to impress me. Thanks for coming alongside me. Brenda, you're loved too.

I'm especially grateful to the team that has invested so much "sweat equity" in this writing project over the past five years: Fred Hitchcock's editing expertise, and Joyce Anderson's and Sarah Moore's diligence and patience with me. Julie Denker's faithful help, Elizabeth Reha's typing of the manuscript, Pat Orton's untiring servant spirit, and Ted Grove's research. A. J. Laubhan, I'm especially appreciative of your leadership of these monthly snapshots called "My Soapbox" and your encouragement to keep writing. And Jerry Wunder, you know that I couldn't have found the time to write if you weren't carrying an incredible load. Thanks again.

Mike High, Joe Battagalia, Steve Farrar, and Jane Anne Smith were all extremely gracious to give me hours of their time in editing and improving the manuscript. Thanks for your solicited editorial comments and concerns. Joe, I am indebted to you for your interest in my writing and our ministry to families.

Thomas Womack's work on the raw manuscript was invaluable. Your gift of polishing a rambling writer's work was extraordinary. I really do appreciate you.

It has been said that a writer is no better than his editorial director and Dan Benson of Here's Life Publishers confirms it. Dan, thanks for your coaching tips, encouragement, and the many hours of sharpening the focus of each chapter. Les Stobbe has never given up on me (and you easily could have). I'm encouraged by your persevering spirit with a demanding author and your belief and energy for this project. Thanks for being willing to take another risk! And to the Here's Life team, thanks for getting *Pulling Weeds, Planting Seeds* into the hands of people who can benefit from it. You did a remarkable job on our first book—your hard work is not taken for granted.

Barbara, no husband could ask for any more in a wife, mother, companion, and friend. Thanks for being you and for believing in me.

And, finally, I want to thank all those who faithfully read "My Soapbox" and who have encouraged me to string these monthly offerings into a book.

Contents

Part III: In My Walk With God

Pulling Weeds, Planting Seeds

Maybe you've experienced the hope of planting a new garden or lawn. You had a snapshot in your mind of what it would look like—a beautiful little vegetable garden neatly edged with blooming annuals and a picket fence, or a lush green *Better Homes and Gardens* lawn that would make your neighbor envious.

And possibly you've felt the backache from hoeing your garden or weeding your plot of turf. Sweating profusely, you wondered if it was worth it.

You found that fruitful gardens and thick, carpet-like lawns don't grow naturally. Weeds do. I wish it weren't so, but it is.

Pulling weeds and planting seeds. It's the story of life. Our lives are individual lots on which either the weeds of selfishness or the fruit of Christlikeness will grow. Jesus taught that the soil of our hearts is the most valuable acreage on planet Earth. For it is from this chunk of terra firma that we uproot weeds, plant good seeds, grow, and harvest fruit for all to see.

Jesus taught about weeds, seeds, and fruitfulness in the parable of the soils in Mark chapter 4. The promise of fruitfulness and the warning of barrenness all depended upon the type of soil (heart) that received the seed (God's Word).

In this parable Jesus warned of the choking influence of thorns, those pesky, prickly weeds which choke and squeeze the life out of fruit-producing seedlings. A farmer friend of mine who grows popcorn once told me that weeds, left unattended, can cut the harvest by as much as 40 percent. As I consider the consequences of "harvest hinderers" in my life, I know I need to get serious about pulling, poisoning, and plowing under weeds.

But I guess the thing that sobers me most about weeds is their tremendous potential for reproduction. When I was a kid I used to take great delight in breaking off a dandelion stem that proudly held a cluster of dandelion seeds. A stiff breeze or puff of breath would instantly launch a jillion of those tiny, angel-hair parachutes. Now, as I fight the spread of similar wind-born warriors in my life and family, I can't help but wonder how many "dandelions" there are in just one wrong choice or ill-spoken word. Scripture warns us that one generation's weeds (sins) can be passed on to as many as four generations. That, my friend, is reproduction.

I wish I had some high-powered nuclear herbicide to help you and me instantly eradicate weeds from our lives. I don't. The reality is the soil in all our lives has weed seeds. What you and I need is a personal visit from the Master Gardener and His hoe.

The following pages were penned to help you uproot the weeds of complacency, selfishness, and spiritual compromise in your life. I hope you will be challenged to take an analysis of the soil of your heart and make a priority of developing and cultivating the rich, fertile soil that is responsive to what God says about life.

I hope you will be compelled to plant seeds that will, as Jesus said, "produce a crop—thirty, sixty, or even a hundred times what was sown." As you read, ask God to do some fresh cultivation in the soil of your heart and to help you pull some weeds and plant some good seeds.

If you do, you'll begin to experience a harvest of confidence, contentment, and character. You have God's Word on it.

A Note To The Reader

The chapters in *Pulling Weeds, Planting Seeds* were originally monthly letters to our Family Life Conference alumni called "My Soapbox" written over the past seven years. Many of our 125,000 alumni have asked me to string these monthly nuggets together and turn them into a book. The chapters are not in sequential order and as a result the ages of our children vary throughout the book. At publication, our six children and their ages are: Ashley 14, Benjamin 13, Samuel 10, Rebecca 8, Deborah 5, and Laura 4.

Pulling Weeds, Planting Seeds

With My Family

1.

Someday When the Kids Are Gone

A wistful glimpse ahead to the "empty nest."

Someday when the kids are gone, there will be plenty of ice cream just for Barbara and me. I won't find the can of Hershey's chocolate on the lower shelf . . . empty and with a sticky bottom. We will return to a small refrigerator and eat on the antique table we used when we were first married.

There won't be those strange-looking leftovers that some kid shoved back in a dark corner of the fridge. And there won't be a teenager standing in front of the refrigerator with a blank look on his face searching for . . . ?

Someday when the kids are gone, we won't have to decipher new words coined by toddlers learning to talk, words like: "hanger-burrs" (hamburgers), "pock-opps" (pockets), "i-camean" (ice cream), "cheros" (Cheerios), "blana" (banana), "banky" (blanket), and "habba-burr day" (happy birthday).

Cars will be clean again. There won't be Sunday school papers, chewed gum, or petrified McDonald's french fries on the floor board.

No diapers. No toys in the tub. No trails of clothing on the floor from the backyard to the upstairs bathtub.

There won't be a jillion tiny things "smushed" in the carpet—gum wrappers, Legos, Matchbox cars, doll combs, fishhooks, ponytail holders, hair barrettes, and Popsicle sticks.

Nor will we stumble over herds of teddy bears, dolls, and stuffed animals grazing or napping on the carpet.

And there won't be nearly as many bills. Bills for the orthodontist, the dentist, many doctors, groceries (ugh), sporting goods store, orthopedic shoes, clothes (thank the Lord for hand-me-downs) and plumbers—retrieving "Froggie," the beanbag who met his fate in the toilet when he got flushed one day.

Someday when the kids are gone, there won't be any more heart-to-heart talks with teens. No more "birds and bees" conversations that caused sweaty palms and blushes—mine and Barbara's. No more grappling over tough decisions—what we should or should not let them do.

Someday when the kids are gone, Barbara and I will go to bed without blank stares on our faces, nearly brain-dead from exhaustion at the end of the day.

Doors, Lights, and Nickels

Doors will be shut.

Cabinet doors in the kitchen will be closed.

And every light in the house won't have to be turned off.

There won't be any jars full of nickels, dimes, and quarters saved for a special trip to Disneyland, the beach, and a Dodgers baseball game.

We won't hear the pitter-patter of little feet running down the hallway and then feel a warm, wiggly body crawling in bed and snuggling with us early on Saturday morning.

Fewer things will be lost, like tools from my garage. No frantic search parties at bedtime for lost blankets. Socks will miraculously find their mates. Car keys will be where they were left. And Barbara's clothes will be in her closet, not in a teenage daughter's dirty clothes hamper.

Fewer things will need to be cleaned, like windows smeared with fingerprints of Sugar Daddies and M&M's; kitchen floors dotted with peanut butter, honey, and apple juice spills; or the side of a garage pelted with mud balls.

Roller Skating in the Kitchen

Someday when the kids are gone, there won't be any popcorn scattered like snow on the living room carpet in front of the television where we watched Dorothy and "The Wizard of Oz" at least twenty-four times. There won't be any roller-skating in the kitchen . . . around the island . . . at dinner time.

Gone will be days of nursing croup, allergies, sore throats, and tummyaches (from too much Halloween candy). No more calendars packed with the agenda of kids: piano lessons, pep rallies, ball practice, art lessons, bunking parties, retreats, or birthday parties.

Perhaps one day the yard will be green again. And without the paraphernalia of glasses, bowls, forks, knives, and spoons carted off by little girls "baking cakes in the sandbox."

One day rooms will be clean. Beds wrinkle-free. And closets neat. And I won't have to apologize and ask a four-year-old's forgiveness for getting angry and impatient.

One day the piercing screams of a two-year-old fighting for survival as the last of six will be replaced with calm conversations where adults talk in a civil manner with one another . . . in complete sentences!

And we won't need nearly as many Band-Aids.

Scrapbooks, Snapshots, and Relics

But there will be memories. Our shelves will be filled with scrapbooks chronicling our family's journey in life—volumes of them, more valuable than any limited-edition, leather-bound bestseller.

Snapshots of vacations. Easter dresses. Winter picnics. A log cabin playhouse that took us forever to build. Fishing and hunting trips. First days of school. Goofing around. Breakfast in bed on birthdays. Family nights. Wiener roasts and s'mores. Christmas traditions. Grandmas, Grandpas, cousins, and friends.

Left behind will be other visible remembrances such as a handmade Father's Day card from a son. A wood plaque titled "World's Best MOM." Assorted crayon drawings, verses, and stick people drawn on construction paper.

Occasionally there will be remembrances of those emotionally churning, frightening, and dramatic moments. Moments like six-year-old Rebecca falling off our twelve-foot deck and landing on her head. Barbara's heart racing at 300 beats a minute when she was three months pregnant with Laura. A lost boy at Disneyland after dark. A scared two-year-old's midnight episode with croup. Ashley, 6, in an oxygen tent, battling asthma in the hospital for four days.

But in the end our home won't be empty. In the words of Bob Benson, Barbara and I "will sit quietly by the fire and listen to the laughter in the walls."

We'll still have the memories—memories that give a sense of fulfillment to parents who grew weary at times, but (hopefully) never lost sight that we were fulfilling God's plan by shaping another generation.

2.

Do Something of Value Tonight

*How those special moments can
plant the seeds of a legacy.*

*D*riving home last night after work I switched on the radio to
catch the news. In a moment of uncharacteristic sincerity,
the announcer made a statement that sliced through my fog of
fatigue.

"I hope you did something of value today. You wasted a whole
day if you didn't."

His statement struck me abruptly. Fortunately, I felt pretty
good about how I had invested my time that day solving some of

the problems of a swiftly growing organization. But in ten minutes I would be home where one lovely lady and six pairs of little eyes would want and need my attention.

Would I do something of value with them tonight?

It's just one night, I thought, *and besides, I'm exhausted.* Then I pondered how one night followed by another, 365 times, adds up to a year. The nights and years seem to be passing with increasing velocity. I thought of our two oldest children, who in only a couple of years would both be drafted into the war of adolescence.

I hope you did something of value today. You wasted a whole day if you didn't. It echoed in my thoughts as I drove through the darkness.

Five minutes more and I'd be home.

I'll bet there are other men like me who are really tired right now. I wondered how they were responding to the question if they heard it. *I bet I do better-than-average with my kids,* I smugly concluded in a moment of pride.

Another question came to mind and lingered. *Did God call me to be merely a better-than-average husband and father? Or to be obedient and to excel?*

To be above average, all you have to do is beat the masses — stay a step ahead of the herd, so to speak. Not much challenge there. But to be obedient and to excel — that means I've got to be a disciple . . . deny myself . . . take up my cross . . . and obey — even when I'm tired and whipped by the day's draining events.

It's just one night. One night. What would I accomplish? Would I waste it spending all evening in front of the television? Or invest it in planting the seeds of a positive legacy?

I wanted "just" one evening of selfishness — to do my own thing. But what if Barbara had a similar attitude? Then who would carry the baton?

What kind of heritage and legacy would I impart? Selfishness?

Or selflessness?

One more minute, and I'd be home.

Just one night, Lord. It's just one night. But then the same angel who wrestled Jacob to the ground pinned me with a half nelson as I drove into the garage.

Okay, I give in. You've got me.

A Right Choice

As the kids surrounded my car like a band of whooping Indians, screaming, "Daddy, Daddy, Daddy," I was glad on this night I had made the right choice.

At supper, rather than just grazing our way through the groceries, we spent a few moments on nostalgia. Each of us answered the question, What was your favorite thing we did as a family this past year?

After supper I gave the kids three choices of what we would do: Play Monopoly together as a family, read a good book together quietly, or wrestle together on the living room floor. Which do you think they chose?

Three little sumo wrestlers grabbed my legs as they began to drag me into the living room. Dad was pinned by the kids. Mom was tickled by Dad. And kids went flying through the air (literally) for the next hour. Even our ten-month-old got in on the act by pouncing on me after she had observed the other kids in action.

Will the kids remember? Maybe, but I doubt it. We didn't break anything to make it memorable. Barbara was thankful for that.

Did they know I had struggled in the car? No.

Did I waste the evening? No. With the power that God supplies, I did my best to leave a legacy that counts—a legacy that will outlive me.

I was reminded of two things. First, I remembered what Paul

wrote in Ephesians 5:15-17: "Therefore be careful how you walk, not as unwise men, but as wise, making the most of your time, because the days are evil. So then do not be foolish, but understand what the will of the Lord is."

Second, I remembered my dad. He was badgered by one determined boy into playing catch over and over again. I can still remember his well-worn mitt and curve ball.

If you struggle as I do with priorities, you might want to commit to memory those verses in Ephesians. The "fool" Paul wrote about is something we never intend to become. It "just happens."

I hope you did something of value today. And I hope you will tonight as well.

3.

Bent Nails and the Freedom to Fail

*Failure is inevitable, but we desperately need
to learn to ask forgiveness of those we wrong.*

I bent nails one Christmas. Five of them in furious, rapid-fire succession. All with my six-year-old son looking on at my exasperation and failure.

It started with a beautiful seven-foot Scotch pine Christmas tree. The problem was its trunk. First it was too big to fit into our "antique" tree stand. Then, after a good deal of whittling, it was too short to reach the bottom of the stand. Only a careful balancing act could keep this tree vertical for any length of time. And with our houseful of children, I decided I didn't want to decorate it and police it twenty-four hours a day. The temptation to my crew of little demolition experts would have been too much.

At the suggestion of my helpful wife, Barbara, I carefully sawed an extension off another log. I then took this lovely tree and attempted to drive just two nails through the one-inch block of wood into the trunk of the tree. Simple plan, right? Wrong.

With a swift blow of the hammer, the first nail bent at a sharp angle as if it were being driven into a prehistoric, petrified Scotch pine. As the second nail followed suit, I began to murmur under my breath that Christmas trees must be a pagan ritual after all.

I calmly walked to the garage and brought back three more nails. I announced to my wife that if I couldn't perform the basic function these nails were intended for, I would burn our beautiful Scotch pine, bent nails and all, in our fireplace and cancel Christmas.

Nail number three was a kissing cousin of nails one and two. With my next brutal blow, number four went into a ninety-degree convulsion. My second tap, more brutal still, caused number four to bound off the porch into the azalea bush. That tree trunk could have been butter and I'm convinced that number five would have bent, which it did. I was furious at the nails, the hammer, the tree, my wife, and Christmas! Do you believe in demon-possessed Christmas trees?

I smashed the end of the tree with the hammer. Hard! (The same way I used to kick a chair, in hopes of punishing it after I had stubbed my toe on it as a kid.) Then I threw the hammer as though it were a javelin and I an Olympic contender and stormed off the porch.

My horrified son, Benjamin, witnessed his Christian father fail with the nails and his emotions. My response was far from Christlike as I threw the tree, flying needles and all, in the trunk of the car with the intent of taking the stupid, pagan, petrified tree back where I got it!

Just this once I should have taken W. C. Field's advice: "If at first you don't succeed—then quit! There's no use being a stupid fool about it!"

Where We Fail the Most

Failure! Who hasn't experienced it? The person who claims he hasn't failed has no standards or goals. He's the biggest failure (and fool) of all. Webster defines failure as: "A falling short; neglect; not succeeding; or a breakdown in operation." That describes a lot of homes and marriages today, doesn't it?

Homes seem to be set up to experience a lot of failure. I think it's because at home, life is so daily, transparent, and visible for all to see. In any home there are only so many rugs to sweep things under, closets to hide things in, and attic spaces to tuck away junk. The honeymoon is over when we run out of space to sweep, hide, and tuck our failures away. That's called reality.

Failures at home come in all sorts of sizes, shapes, and weights.

There are the light, small ones called mistakes, errors, or goofs, like breaking a piece of china, spilling catsup on a new shirt, ripping your jeans, stepping on your wife's foot (with golf shoes), or failing to carry the garbage out.

There are the heavier, medium-sized packages of failure that hurt a little deeper. Shouting at the kids (for the fourth time in one day), having your kid bring home a *D* or *F* on a report card, or habitually promising something to your kids and then going back on the promise.

Then there are the cumbersome and heaviest of failures that leave us feeling crushed under the weight. A divorce, a strained relationship, a rebellious teenager who thinks he is always right, battering your wife physically or verbally, or failing to lead your wife and children spiritually.

But the biggest failure of all is a wasted life, a mediocre life, lived outside of God's will. Elton Trueblood made this statement: "Mediocrity is a heresy and a sin. To make your life small when it could be great is a sin of the worst magnitude."

Mediocrity in a human life comes in two bitter flavors: one that flagrantly disobeys God's laws, and another that just ignores them. Lots of Christians suffer in one of these two camps. Isaiah spoke of this when he wrote, "All of us like sheep have gone astray, each of us has turned to his own way." We can go our own way and be disobedient, leaving the laws and principles of Scriptures that we know to be true. The man or woman who goes his own way cannot be the husband or wife or parent God intended him or her to be. We can also go our own way through neglect: We may still be attending church, singing songs and saying the right things, while neglecting our personal walk with God.

One of the crucial areas in which we must help our children is learning to deal with failure. Next time you fail, think of Peter, who failed Christ three times, but who received forgiveness at the foot of the cross. Christ stands ready to forgive all. One absolutely essential ingredient in every Christian home is a contrite heart. You will never receive forgiveness for failure from God or people unless your heart has been broken and you've asked for forgiveness. The heart of one who asks his mate, "Will you forgive me?" or his children, "Hey, I blew it. Will you please forgive me?" (as I had to do with Benjamin after my wrestling match with the Christmas tree), is the heart that will receive forgiveness in full. There is no use living a life of mediocrity.

The next time you see a bent nail, thank Jesus Christ that He hasn't quit on us and He hasn't let you quit! Someday in heaven He'll straighten all those nails and cause Christmas trees to have the right-sized trunks. Guaranteed! But in the meantime, allow yourself the freedom to fail—constructively! Learn from your failures. Be swift to ask forgiveness of those you may have offended. The positive example you set for your family will serve as a bond to draw you even more closely together.

4.

Dad's Home!

A tribute to a father who "took the time."

Dad's home!" I used to yell as I heard the back door slam.

Our small, two-story frame house would reverberate loudly when Dad came in and slammed the back door behind him. It was his signature and signal that a day of work was completed, and a man was now home.

I would dash down the hall and through the kitchen to greet him with a well-deserved hug, then follow him like a little puppy to the wash room where he washed his calloused and grimy hands. Everything about him signaled that he was a "real man" — from the gritty Lava soap he used to the Vitalis hair tonic and Old Spice after-shave.

My dad was a unique blend of no-nonsense and discipline with a subtle sense of humor. He was a quiet and private man. He didn't seem to need many words to get the job done. His countenance commanded respect. In fact, several boys had a personality trans- formation when they graduated from the third-grade Sunday school class to my Dad's fourth-grade class. Miraculously, dis- cipline problems dried up along with dozens of paper spit-wads. In the twelve months that followed, paper airplanes were grounded and eight boys sat up straight in their chairs, listening dutifully to the lesson.

Curves, Sliders, Knuckle-balls

"Hook" Rainey, they used to call him. The tall lefty got his nickname from his curve ball—a pitch so crooked it mystified bat- ters. I got the feeling he was on his way to becoming a legend in his day—he even pitched a game against Dizzy Dean. Funny thing, but he could never remember the score of that memorable game! I used to accuse him of convenient amnesia.

I recall the easy chair that used to carry the shape of his ex- hausted form. It was as he was reading the evening paper that I usually planned my assault on him. I'm certain I nearly pestered him to death on more than one occasion while asking my weary dad to play catch. And play catch he did. Night after night, Dad taught me how to throw a curve, slider, and knuckle-ball. He used to claim you could count the stitches on his knuckle-ball as it ap- proached without a spin—and when he threw that patented knuckler the entire front yard was filled with laughter—his and mine. I always loved to hear him laugh. Somehow it told me that everything was secure.

When I was three or so, he went hunting in Colorado and "bagged" a fierce teddy bear. He staged the "action" on film and brought the "slain" beast back to me. My kids now play with that worn out thirty-five-year-old black-and-white bear.

I watched him look after the needs of his mother — he used to visit his mom three or four times a week. He modeled what it meant to "honor one's parents."

From him I learned about integrity, trust, and how to be a man of my word. His example taught me the importance of perseverance, for he stuck with his job for nearly forty-five years. The indelible impression he has left on me is that of sinking roots down deep — and living in a small community with the same people with whom he did business.

When I was in high school, I won a magazine sales contest because I introduced myself as Hook Rainey's son. That was good enough for an instant sale for nearly all of my customers. My dad had helped so many people that being his son gave me immeasurable credibility. (For a while I actually thought I was a great salesman!)

His reputation was untarnished. His funeral was attended by nearly a third of the people in our small southwest Missouri community where he had lived and done his work for his entire life, all within five miles of his birthplace. One man was even able to say about my father, "In all my years I never heard a negative word about Hook Rainey."

Making Memories

Instead of just things, he gave me imperishable memories. Little league baseball the three years he was my coach. Fishing trips where he netted my fish. A "clipped" collection of all the baseball and basketball scores from my games, of which he never missed one. There are memories of watching him through the frosted window of our old pickup truck as he delivered hams at Christmas. Memories of the feel of his whiskers when he wrestled with me on the floor of the living room. Memories of him whispering to me, an extroverted, impetuous boy, not to bother people while they work. And memories of snuggling close to him as we watched the baseball game of the week on television with Dizzy Dean as the announcer.

As an impressionable young boy, my radar caught more of his

life than he ever knew. During my perilous teenage years he was the model and hero I needed — and he still is. He taught me the importance of hard work and completing a task. I learned about lasting commitment from him — I never feared my parents would divorce. My dad was absolutely committed to my mom. I felt secure and protected.

Most importantly, he taught me about *character*. He did what was right, even when no one was looking. I never heard him talk about cheating on taxes — he paid them and didn't grumble. His integrity was impeccable. I never heard him lie, and his eyes always demanded the same truth in return. The mental image of his character still fuels and energizes my life today.

"Dad's home!" I can still hear the door slam, and feel the house quake.

This morning as I write this, Dad truly is "home" — in heaven. I look forward to seeing him again someday and thanking him for the legacy he gave me.

But right now, you'll have to pardon me — I miss him.

5.

Best Homes and Gardens

Neatness? Tranquility? Meet a <u>real</u> Christian family.

I don't often look at *Better Homes and Gardens* or other magazines like it, with their photos of homes that have "the look"—neatness, tranquility, and order. When I see those magazines it fouls up my sense of reality. At our house, the second law of thermodynamics—which says everything in the universe is moving from order to disorder—is fully operative.

The other day, however, I came home to find a model family. The children were bathed and waiting patiently at the supper table. No sibling rivalry. No tattling. No roller-derby in the kitchen while I tried to talk with Barbara. The meal was enjoyable, the conversation pleasant. *Better Homes and Gardens* should have had a photographer there.

It was exactly the way everyone expects us to be, but the way we seldom are. It was an exception, not a rule. You see, we are a normal Christian family. To find out what a normal Christian family is, listen to these descriptions of a more "typical day" at the Raineys.

I came home from work one day to find a garbage disposal clogged by a foreign object that had been tossed into its guts by some small creature (I think we call them toddlers). Only after squishing through mushy apple peels and who knows what else did my hand retrieve the object. Also, the dishwasher had shorted out and wouldn't finish its cycle. Inside it, large chunks of food were stuck as if with super-glue to the dishes' glazed finish. A chisel, not soap, was now needed.

It had been a horrible, terrible, no-good, very bad day for Barbara, and she was impatient and grumpy to prove it. Our three-year-old was sick, the house was dirty, Cheerios were all over the floor, and our twelve-month-old had her fist full of chocolate chips . . . melting chocolate chips. (Later, I found her scavenging the scattered Cheerios from the floor.) Our five-year-old was still recovering from a broken arm suffered from a fall off a trampoline. Meanwhile the oldest two, who were ten and eight, complained in unison of tummyaches. What a welcome!

Someone has said, "A clean house is a sign of a life misspent." I have also heard it said that "You can't raise grass and children simultaneously." Yet I sometimes lose the right perspective, and feel our children get in the way of us having a happy home!

"Eat All You Can Eat Cafe"

It's tough at times to balance the hectic demands of raising kids with the proper values for calmness and order that we want to instill in our children. But the bonuses for trying to maintain the balance are there, too. Not too long ago we had a reward. The children served Barbara and me an "elegant" meal. The gourmet menu was hand-crafted out of construction paper. The name of the exclusive establishment in which we dined (our living room) was the "Eat All You Can Eat Cafe."

At the "Eat All You Can Eat Cafe," we enjoyed juice, a Jell-O salad, our choice of hot dogs or macaroni and cheese, and toast (taking our chances on what color it would be). The service was absolutely impeccable. Smiling children waited on us with towels draped over their arms, big grins, polite thank yous, and even the shunning of a tip after the meal. They were thrilled that they could serve Mom and Dad in this way.

These contrasting stories represent reality in the life of one family — a very large but normal family, and a family that is learning much.

We are learning that selfish people don't last long in relationships. Going my own way makes big waves in a small pond.

We are learning to be authentic, to admit we're wrong . . . more than just occasionally. At our place, slippery people who try to cop out when they are wrong get nailed. The truth is important.

Respect for each other is becoming a buzz word around our house. When one of us yells at another, we try to consider how that makes the other feel.

We're also trying to give generous portions of praise to one another. Not that we always do it, but we've found that when we praise other family members for *who they are* and *what they do right,* it makes home a much more pleasant place to live.

Real People

Finally, we're seeing that we are not very good listeners. Personally, I really feel like a failure most of the time, but I'm learning. How can a child become like Christ if no one listens to him? How can a couple be real if neither mate asks a question or ponders the answer?

An authentic, normal Christian family isn't perfect; in fact, it's nowhere near perfection. It simply has too many egos that are in the process of putting self to death so Jesus Christ might live His life through them.

The world today is crying out for real people who live in real families, and who represent a real God who has given them something real — something better than *Better Homes and Gardens*.

So here's to smudged windows, sticky floors splattered with apple juice, disagreements, sibling rivalry, and noise — produced by family members developing character as they are becoming like Jesus Christ. After all, real homes are the best!

6.

A Recipe for Memories

*Do something today to plant the seeds
of a special family memory.*

Our home sits on the western edge of a quiet wooded ridge that overlooks a sky-blue lake. Beyond the lake are ten ranges of oak- and pine-covered hills that provide the final resting place for the sun each evening. Our "tribe" often gathers on the back porch to watch the sun sink behind those hills. It's postcard-perfect. Yet the house and its spectacular setting — the woods, the hills, and the lake — don't make it a home. It's the people who live there and the memories we've made together.

First, there is the memory of one of the kids' business ventures—KIDS KOOKIES INKORPORATED. Move over, Mrs. Fields. These freshly baked diet-busters, ninety-five cents a dozen, are made from the finest ingredients. The children even wash their hands before making them! They set up their portable business at a busy fork in the road about a mile from our home.

In addition to KIDS KOOKIES, they raffled off some good Christian books and tapes. They have a heart for a profit, but above all they want to use their business to get the word out about Christ. They care about the eternal destiny of people. (The extent of their concern puts Mom and Dad in the shade sometimes.)

We also created great memories with a blue-ribbon fishing vacation during a recent summer. For eight days we parked our car beside our cabin and didn't move it—a record. The rainbow trout in the lake smashed our lures. And Ashley, our oldest daughter, even won first prize in a local fishing contest with her four-pound, four-ounce German brown trout. We made that old trout a permanent memory—on her wall!

Shimmering Stars, Roaring Fires

Then there was a horseback ride with friends to the top of a 9800-foot peak. We enjoyed a picnic at the top among wildflowers as tall as the horses bridles. Benjamin learned something about being a cowpoke: He was bucked off (no permanent injuries). The high altitude meant crisp July evenings filled with millions of shimmering stars, roaring fires, and memories that will last long after the photos have faded.

Sometimes memories are found in very simple packages, like a note I found scrawled across a three-hole-punched school paper. One of our children had scribbled a prayer of confession: "Dear God: Please help me not to be rebellious at other peoples things." No "snowing" God here. Just honest words, straight from the heart.

There's also a memory of mischief when I caught our two-year-old with her hand and arm in the cookie jar and her face smeared with the evidence of chocolate chips. "Me didn't do it,

Daddy," she said, "Me didn't do it."

I remember cherished romantic moments with Barbara. Periodically we put Ashley and Benjamin in charge of the children upstairs and we enjoy our special meal downstairs.

Even when our special meals are interrupted, it's pretty difficult to get irritated at a blue-eyed, sandy-haired boy who wants a good-night kiss from his dad. I hope he never gets too old for that. Wanting to get in on her seven-year-old brother's smooching action, our four-year-old trotted down the steps for her portion. Kisses and hugs are not tightly rationed here. When I help Barbara get them tucked into bed, I get down on my knees and pray. I want them to remember me as a father who prayed for them.

The Last Diaper

Another special memory is the day the last disposable diaper was passed out in the Rainey household—after twelve years of being a faithful consumer of Pampers. No, we didn't have the diaper bronzed.

It has been said that God gave us memories so we could smell roses in December. I'll never forget the smell of a newborn, or the feel of a baby's soft cheeks and tummy. I'll miss it a little, but maybe someday a grandbaby will recall those coos and grins forever stored in my memory.

If you haven't done something wild and crazy recently to make a memory with your kids, do it tonight. Oh yes—don't forget to take a picture of it!

7.

Somebody's Mom

"The virtues of a mother shall be visited on her children."
— Charles Dickens

When she was thirty-five, she carried him in her womb while he did his best to kick out her slats (ribs). It was not easy being a mother in 1948. After nine long months he was finally born. Breech. A difficult, dangerous birth. She still says, "He came out feet first, hit the floor running, and he's been running ever since." Affectionately she calls him "The Roadrunner."

There were no dishwashers and no disposable diapers, and only crude washing machines. But she faithfully gave herself to the task as year followed year. She nursed him through dozens of colds and sore throats and bouts of flu, chicken pox, mumps, and measles. She always offered a chilled washcloth on his forehead when his fever was high. Her steaming-hot potato soup always tasted best to him when he was propped against a pillow in bed.

A warm kitchen was her trademark — the most secure place in the home, a shelter in the storm. Her small but tidy kitchen always attracted a crowd. It was the place where food and friends were made! She was a good listener. She always seemed to have time.

Two-Thousand Calories Per Bite

Delicious smells used to drift out of that kitchen — the aroma of a juicy cheeseburger drew him like a magnet from the "north bedroom." (Wendy's didn't invent the first "thick and juicy" burger — this mom did.) There were green beans seasoned with hickory-smoked bacon grease. Sugar cookies. Pecan pie. And best of all, chocolate bon-bons — made only at Christmas, and with two-thousand calories in each bite.

She wasn't perfect. He never lets her forget about the time she was talking on the phone and he was beating pans together, as three-year-olds naturally like to do. She impatiently threw a pencil at him. Much to her shock, it narrowly missed his eye and left a sliver of lead in his cheek that is still there.

And once, when he was five, she tied him to his bed. He had thrown a gun at his brother, but it missed him and instead hit her prized antique vase. The vase developed a split personality as it broke into a few hundred pieces. Three months later, through a toothless grin, he embarrassed his mom by stretching the story. He announced at their favorite restaurant to the family's favorite waitress, "My Mom's had me tied up for 'free' (three) months!"

But she taught him forgiveness by forgiving him an infinite number of times for not making his bed and not picking up his clothes. She also forgave him when as a teenager he got angry and took a swing at her (and fortunately missed).

Tough Loyalty

The most profound thing she modeled was a love for God and people. Compassion was always her companion. She taught him about giving to others even when she didn't feel like it. She also taught him about accountability, truthfulness, honesty, and transparency. She modeled a tough loyalty to his dad. He always knew divorce was never an option for them.

She took care of her own parents when old age took its toll. She also went to church . . . faithfully. In fact, she led this six-year-old boy to Christ in her Bible study class one Sunday evening.

Even today, her age doesn't stop her from fishing in a cold rain with her son. Nor does her age stop them from running off together to get Chinese food, or from "wolfing down" a cheeseburger and a dozen chocolate bon-bons—laughing all the time.

She's truly a woman to be honored.

She's more than somebody's mother . . . she's my Mom.

Mom, I love you.

"Honor your father and your mother, as the Lord your God has commanded you, that your days may be prolonged, and that it may go well with you in the land which the Lord your God gives you" (Deuteronomy 5:16).

8.

Spinning Plates and Broken People

A man's priorities.

A motto I heard recently goes like this:

WINNERS CONCENTRATE ON WINNING
WHILE LOSERS CONCENTRATE ON JUST GETTING BY

If that statement were carved in granite at the headquarters of a Fortune 500 company, you would nod your head in agreement. Inwardly you might say, "Now that's the way to run a business. I'm sure this company is truly a company of excellence. They know how to do things right!"

Yet when it comes to the family, most homes today have to

be characterized as losers. Too many marriages have become marred by mediocrity. Children are seen, at best, as a status symbol—our way to achieve something through them that we weren't able to achieve when we were their age.

Too many marriages today are concentrating on "just getting by." With that as the goal, it is no wonder so many marriages don't amount to much.

Denis Waitley, in his bestseller *The Seeds of Greatness,* tells the story of his grandmother whom he idolized. She crossed an apricot and a plum tree and called it a plumcot. This delicious fruit was perfected by the gentle, wise old lady after careful and tedious pruning and grafting of the two fruit-bearing trees.

As a boy, Waitley learned a valuable lesson from his grandmother. She harvested a plumcot because that was what she planted.

Marriage is a lot like that—we never get out of a marriage what we do not put into it.

One man confessed, "At work I concentrate on winning, and as a result, I am a winner. At home, however, I concentrate on just getting by."

It's no wonder he was losing at home.

Winning Where It Counts?

As Americans, we think of ourselves as winners . . . we are used to winning, but all too often we're winning in the wrong places. As a result, we may end up losing in the most important place . . . home.

Vance Havner, commenting on our misplaced priorities, has said: "Americans know the price of everything, but the value of nothing."

If a business goes bankrupt, it is the president or the chairman of the board who is to blame. Similarly, if the home fails, you and I as husbands and fathers are to blame. You and I must master the ageless art of leadership and apply it to our families. If we ever hope to win at home, we must focus on winning.

But too many of us, as the leaders of our families, are like the man who used to come on the "Ed Sullivan Show" years ago and spin the plates. He would start at one end of a long table and place a stick perpendicular to the table then spin a plate on the stick. In consecutive order the plates would be placed on sticks and spun — two, three, four, five, six plates. As the first plate slowed down, it would begin to wobble. I can remember feeling the urge to want to jump through the TV and help the man by grabbing the plate before it fell off the stick and shattered into tiny slivers. But the man would rush back and expertly spin the first plate again as the audience breathed a sigh of relief.

On he would go . . . seven, eight, nine plates. By this time, plates two, three, and four were now beginning to wobble. And just before you knew everything would come crashing down, he would quickly scoop up all of the plates in his professional hands as if he were carrying them to the cupboard, then bow to the applause of the audience.

Losing Our Focus

Similarly, the roles we assume in life as husband, father, businessman, civic leader, church leader, golfer, fisherman — all represent different plates in our lives. We begin spinning them early in our married life, with plate number one being our marriage. Receiving our focused attention, the plate spins along merrily and does well. With the addition of plates number two (our business) and three (children), efforts to focus become more difficult. We keep adding plates until we finally step back from the table and see that two or three of the first plates are beginning to wobble badly. We have to make choices. Decisions. Decisions based on priorities. Our family has needs, but we mistakenly choose to meet more material "needs" by applying our efforts primarily to our business. The result: Focus is lost, and important plates fall and shatter.

However, most businessmen are not worried about starving. Most of us are concerned about status, significance, accumulation of "more," and how we can feed the materialistic monster that lives within us. A good friend recently said, "Materialism is not what you have, it is what has you."

Too many husbands and fathers have become dizzy by the many spinning plates we have set up. We give our family an occasional spin just to keep things at "status quo." We focus on just getting by.

The result? More plates begin to fall off the table. Children become strangers — children who are crying out for attention. Our wives plead for help. Meanwhile, being the visionary leaders that we are, we ignore fallen plates and continue adding others. Yet the psalmist warns, "Unless the Lord build the house, they labor in vain who build it" (Psalm 127:1).

There is no question why so many marriages and families are functioning poorly. Nothing that is alive — a business, a school, a basketball team, or a family — can function without leadership that expends energy, time, and — most importantly — focused attention. Without these, the plates will begin to fall.

"How Many Plates Are Enough?"

Being somewhat a selfish man myself, there is nothing I would love better than to have my dozen ego-stroking plates spinning in addition to my family plates. However, I am constantly directed by Jesus Christ to come to grips with my limits. I have been wrestled to the ground by Him on more than one occasion, and forced to answer the question, "How many plates can you keep spinning and still win? How much is enough?"

Another question which redirects me is, "Where do I want to win so badly that I am unequivocally unwilling to lose?"

"And which of all those other plates would I be willing to lose for the sake of my family, if need be?"

Today tough questions face Christian businessmen and

leaders. We have created a cult of Christian celebrities. We worship successful businessmen and pro athletes who can perform in the office or on the field. We pay little regard to whether they are a success in their personal and private lives. The time has come for a new breed of Christian husbands and fathers.

We need a new breed who will say "No" to more bucks when it means sacrificing their family. A new breed who will ask this question along with every decision they make: "How will this affect my relationships within the family?" A new breed of man who will recognize that he needs to leave something to posterity that will outlive him . . . proven character in his children. A new breed of leaders who realize that to succeed in the eyes of men, but fail in the eyes of God, is the ultimate failure.

One man has said, "It is better to fail in a cause that will ultimately succeed than to succeed in a cause that will ultimately fail."

One last question: Will you take upon yourself the challenge Albert Einstein gave a group of young scientists? While addressing this highly motivated group of young men, he said, "Gentlemen, try not to become men of success. But rather, try to become men of value."

9.

Three of the Most Difficult Words to Admit

Beware of living independently of one another.

I used to think the most difficult words to utter were, "I love you."

I remember, as a typically ungrateful, unexpressive teenager, the first time I told my mom and dad "I love you." Looking my parents in the eye and saying those three words was excruciating.

Then there was the first time I told Barbara I loved her — my heart jumped wildly, and my adrenaline was the only thing flowing faster than the beads of sweat on my forehead. Whew! I remember wondering how young couples in love could survive the experience!

Telling another person "I love you" represents risk and vulnerability. Yet however difficult those words of love may be, three other words are even more arduous to express. They are:

I *NEED* YOU.

Consider the number of people you have expressed your love to: your mate, children, parents, extended family, and possibly a few select friends.

Now think of those to whom you have said, "I need you" — a much smaller number, most likely. But why?

Most of us have difficulty admitting need. It means we are dependent upon another. It means we are less than complete by ourselves. We may even feel that our mate is burdened enough already — "Why should I weigh her down further with my needs?" we reason inwardly.

It's interesting that in Genesis 2:18 Adam had to be told he had a need. God said, "It is not good for man to be alone." And even after that divine authoritative statement, Adam had to name a few million creatures to finally get the point: *He needed something — someone!*

Today is no different — it still takes God to show us how we need our mates.

True partnerships are cemented as couples frequently and specifically verbalize their need of one another.

But at some point in time between the walk down the wedding aisle and the fifth anniversary, a thief often makes off with our mutual admission of interdependence. In fact, it's ironic that marriage, the ultimate declaration of one person's need for another, would end up being an accomplice to the thief.

Think Back on the Romance

Think back to those early days of romance and intrigue. She made you laugh. He made you feel secure and stable. She brought warmth into a room, instantly and mystically. His sensitivity made you realize how others feel and think. You needed your mate because he or she:

- stopped to smell the roses that you didn't even notice were there.
- made art galleries and museums come alive. (Earlier, you nearly flunked first-grade finger-painting, and you believed people died daily of boredom in those cold, dank, sterile, marble buildings. But now it is different.)
- made you laugh, when you wanted to cry.
- was organized and you weren't.
- shared openly and honestly about emotions while you had locked up your feelings for years.
- listened when you really needed someone to listen to you.

Perhaps most importantly, you needed to feel valued and important. You needed to be *needed*. Here was another person who authentically admitted he or she needed to spend the rest of his or her life with you, and that need made you feel significant.

Maybe today you and your mate act like you don't need each other.

Perhaps you have lost sight of "how" you need your mate. Your marriage is heading down an alley that dead-ends in dark despair—the loneliness of a life shared with no one. But there's hope.

"I Need You..."

Let me jog your memory of ways you need each other. Why not put a check beside each one that is appropriate to you—then, express to your mate you need him or her:

1. For a balanced and truthful view of yourself. Who else knows you as well and can give you an honest perspective (and con-

tinue to offer you acceptance) when you need it most?

2. For a full-color view of life. For me, life without Barbara would be at best a foggy black-and-white experience. She adds intense splashes of rich colors and lively and contrasting tints to life. She brings a different way to view and experience the panorama. I *need* her! Your mate undoubtedly looks at life through a different set of lenses than you do. You are a broader person because of those differences — why try to change them, when you need them?

3. To believe in you when others don't and you can't. We need another who is a mirror of positive acceptance, expectancy, praise, and the belief that we are indeed a person who is significant.

4. To multiply your laughter, share your tears, add his experience with God to yours, and help you subtract your haunting past from your life.

5. To put the brakes on when you are trying to accelerate too fast or about to go off a cliff. And to encourage you to "risk it" when you'd rather not.

6. To raise healthy and balanced children. Two people temper one another's weaknesses, complement each other's blind spots, and help reinforce each other's strong points as they raise children together.

7. To draw you out when you need to talk, but don't want to. You need a mate who will force you to be authentic and honest with your emotions, and not let you retreat to solitary confinement and bury your fears, anger, disappointment, or hurt.

8. To be an unpredictable romanticist, even when you prefer the routines of the ruts.

9. To help when times are rugged. God meant for our burdens to be shared — carried together, not single-handedly. By asking for help you may get more than just a pair of hands — you may get an understanding, compassionate heart.

Beware of living independently of one another. Sure, you're both busy. Yet sometimes busy people build their lives around activities only to find years later that they are alone. Imprisoned by selfishness and a failure to take risks, they are living independently of the person God has sovereignly given them to share life with.

A Practical Project for Tonight

So what can you do today? How about completing this project with your mate after dinner tonight:

On a sheet of paper, list five to ten specific ways you need your mate . . . something more than laundry, paycheck, meals—and yes, sex (unless that would really surprise your mate!).

Now use your list to compose a letter expressing your need of your mate. Or take a long walk together and share the ways you need him or her. But don't just read your list. A tender touch and eye-to-eye expression will make it more meaningful.

You really do *need* your mate.

10.
Pistol
Lips

Hurtful words are like weeds in your family garden.
Pull them, and plant seeds of affirmation.

Did you know you have an arsenal of weapons right under your nose? "What kind of weapons?" you ask. "Swords? Rocket launchers? Pistols? Machine guns?"

No. But you do have a formidable arsenal of words—words which when fired in rapid succession are capable of destroying, and words which when delivered carefully, gently, and strategically can initiate peace and fortify character. This cadre of strategic arms is found right under your nose within the power of your tongue. But before I tell you about this arsenal let me tell you about a man whose artillery was not words, but his arm and a ball.

From the dugout you notice his cheek is bulging with a hefty chew of Redman, and his forehead is covered with sweat as he takes his first of eight warm-up pitches. As you prepare to hit against this notoriously "wild" pitcher, you notice that his first pitch sails over the catcher's head and slams into the screen. His next errant pitch burrows wildly in the dirt and bounces up, nearly hitting you in the on-deck circle some twenty feet to the side of home plate.

Nervous and uncertain about the direction of the next little white pellet, you take your turn in the batter's box. You are very loose. Swinging three times at ninety-plus-miles-per-hour fastballs, you bail out and eagerly trot back to the safety of your dugout.

Who was that pitcher? He was former New York Yankee pitcher Ryne Duren, known as the patron saint of the "psyche-out." Duren knew how to mentally harass opposing batters with an assortment of wildly launched pitches and schemes that left the batter terrified.

Only after finishing his career did Duren confess to the ploy. "When I would warm up in the bullpen, I used to throw toward the opposing team's dugout. I always managed to allow at least one pitch to carom into their dugout, giving them fair warning of who was to become the relief pitcher." With a sly grin he added, "On occasion, I missed home plate so badly, I almost hit the guy some twenty feet away in the on-deck circle."

Words of Intimidation

Duren knew he could use the same baseball that batters were trying to hit to intimidate them from performing their intended purpose. And just as Ryne Duren used his arm and the baseball as his arsenal of intimidation, we use our tongue and the words it hurls as weapons to inflict fear, pain, and guilt on others.

What kind of "hurler" are you?

Do you hurl intimidating words that leave your mate

paralyzed and unable to respond? You know, the kind of words that bring your mate down, or leave him defenseless? Joseph Conrad once noted, "There is a weird power in the spoken word." How do you use this "weird power" with your mate?

I'm reminded of a spiteful relationship between Winston Churchill and Lady Astor. They repeatedly expressed their contempt for one another. One day Lady Astor said to him, "Mr. Prime Minister, if you were my husband I'd poison your drink." Churchill was equal to the occasion when he sharply replied, "Well, if you were my wife, I'd drink it!"

On another occasion she found Churchill had been drinking a little too freely. "Mr. Prime Minister," she scolded, "I perceive you are drunk!" He smiled and wryly replied, "Yes, Lady Astor, and you are ugly. But tomorrow I shall be sober!"

Maybe you are like Lady Astor and you've met your match. You frequently hurl poisonous words in an attempt to hurt another person. Or possibly you are like Churchill, always needing to win by getting in the last word.

Regardless, let's consider what can happen when we move our tongue and words from the attack mode to the peace mode using the power of the tongue for good. Good words can fortify another's confidence. They can express belief. They can give hope, vision, praise, and encouragement.

Words of Encouragement

In our book *Building Your Mate's Self-Esteem,* Barbara and I wrote of ten building blocks to build your mate's self-image. One of those building blocks is the *power of words.* Words that express belief in another can be the fuel that gets your mate through a "wilderness experience" — words which help him or her deal with the plague of self-doubt.

In our book we share a story that graphically illustrates our need for another's positive words and belief in our life. It is a story from the book *In His Image,* in which Dr. Paul Brand tells of his experience as a surgeon in London during World War II.

Peter Foster was a Royal Air Force pilot. These men (pilots) were the cream of the crop of England — the brightest, healthiest, most confident and dedicated, and often the most handsome men in the country. When they walked the streets in their decorated uniforms, the population treated them as gods. All eyes turned their way. Girls envied those who were fortunate enough to walk beside a man in Air Force blue.

However, the scene in London was far from romantic, for the Germans were attacking relentlessly. Fifty-seven consecutive nights they bombed London. In waves of 250, some 1500 bombers would come each evening and pound the city.

The RAF Hurricanes and Spitfires that pilots like Foster flew, looked like mosquitoes pestering the huge German bombers. The Hurricane was agile and effective, yet it had one fatal design flaw. The single propeller engine was mounted in front, a scant foot or so from the cockpit, and the fuel lines snaked alongside the cockpit toward the engine. In a direct hit, the cockpit would erupt in an inferno of flames. The pilot could eject, but in the one or two seconds it took him to find the lever, heat would melt off every feature of his face: his nose, his eyelids, his lips, often his cheeks.

These RAF heroes many times would undergo a series of twenty to forty surgeries to refashion what once was their face. Plastic surgeons worked miracles, yet what remained of the face was essentially a scar.

Peter Foster became one of those "downed pilots." After numerous surgical procedures, what remained of his face was indescribable. The mirror he peered into daily couldn't hide the facts. As the day for his release from the hospital grew closer, so did Peter's anxiety about being accepted by his family and friends.

He knew that one group of airmen with similar injuries had returned home only to be rejected by their wives and girlfriends. Some of the men were divorced by wives who were unable to accept this new outer image of their husband. Some men became recluses, refusing to leave their houses.

In contrast, there was another group who returned home to families who gave loving assurance of acceptance and continued worth. Many became executives and professionals, leaders in their communities.

Peter Foster was in that second group. His girlfriend assured him that nothing had changed except a few millimeters' thickness of skin. She loved him, not for his facial membrane, she assured him. The two were married just before Peter left the hospital.

"She became my mirror," Peter said of his wife. "She gave me a new image of myself. Even now, regardless of how I feel, when I look at her she gives me a warm, loving smile. That tells me I am OK," he says confidently.[1]

Did you know that your words can have a powerful impact on your mate? Like Peter Foster's wife, you *can* use your words to express loving acceptance and thereby reduce the fears and rejections of life. Your words may be the missing antibiotic for your mate's self-doubt. Even today, more than forty years after the war, countless buildings throughout Europe bear the scars of German artillery. Does your mate still carry any scars that others — or you — may have left?

Solomon offers an appropriate piece of advice: "A word fitly spoken is like apples of gold in settings of silver" (Proverbs 25:11, NIV). Why don't you pack a "golden delicious" in your mate's lunch today? How about a brief note simply saying "I love you"? Your mate needs you on his team, not on his case. Find something good to say to your mate today and every day.

P.S. This applies to your children, too.

1. Dr. Paul Brand and Philip Yancey, *In His Image* (Grand Rapids, MI: Zondervan Publishing House, 1984). Used by permission.

11.

Lights Out!

Pulling the weed of complacency,
planting the seed of romance.

Do you remember the day of President Kennedy's assassination? I can describe the room I was in, the people who were there, and what the weather was like outside. Hearing the news of his death was like being struck repeatedly with an emotional sledgehammer that pounded the spikes of grief, fear, and confusion into a fourteen-year-old boy's heart. I'll never forget that day.

Twenty-five years later another day brought news that pierced my heart. No visible bullet was fired. There was no assassin at whom I could vent my anger. There was only the word that a hero of mine had fallen. His spiritual influence had been tarnished by adultery. I was nauseated when the news came, for I had drunk deeply from the well of his writings, his preaching, and his life.

I've done a lot of thinking since then.

I've pondered the tragedy to his ministry. I've winced at the shame to him, to his family, and to the name of Christ. I've asked myself, *How many like him must fall before we who are Christians come out of our sanctified closets and admit that sexual temptations do exist?* And I've grappled over the growing number of Christians who've lost their marriages, families, and ministries due to sexual infidelity.

As a result, I have determined that we need to start asking one another some tough questions. Like a man asking another man, "Are you being the leader of your family and taking care of your wife's needs—spiritually, emotionally, and sexually?" "Are you being faithful sexually to your wife?" "Are you being faithful mentally?" "Are you reading anything that you shouldn't?"

And woman to woman: "Are you sending your husband into the world hungry, with his sexual needs unmet?" "Are you a 'marriage bed magnet' who causes him to daydream at work about you?"

I know this isn't the entire solution, but I have concluded that it's time we stop assuming we are all beyond temptation, and start exhorting husbands and wives to pay more attention to satisfying one another's physical and emotional needs.

For some, any open admission about the sexual dimension of life is strictly taboo. But as Dr. Howard Hendricks says, "We should not be ashamed to discuss that which God was not ashamed to create."

If God isn't blushing about what takes place in our bedrooms, then why are we? Why is it that many of us feel so uncomfortable talking about sex? Why are we so afraid of this God-created portion of our personhood? Is it because we feel so uncomfortable with our sexuality?

"GP" for an Affair-proof Marriage

This chapter is rated "GP" for "God's Plan" — seven exhortations to "affair-proof" your marriage.

1. *Make your marriage bed your priority.* Exhaustion is the great zapper of passion. Our already tired blood is further thinned by feverishly packed schedules. The result is that we have little time and energy to share, give, or receive. Fatigue does not fuel passion.

Practically, some couples could go their own independent way indefinitely, denying their need for one another. But God gave us sex as a drive to merge, to force us out of our isolation.

Am I suggesting that you write "sex" down on your calendar? I'll let you decide. But some who read this don't need a tablespoon of Geritol — you just need to say "no" to some good things and go to bed early — about 8:00 P.M. or so.

2. *Talk together about what pleases one another.* Just last month I spoke to a group of wives whose husbands are in the ministry. During the message I took a few minutes to address the subject of intimacy and how so many men bomb out of the ministry because of sexual sin.

Afterward, a young wife came up to tell me about a conversation she had had with her husband. As they were driving home after he had spoken at church one night, she turned to him and asked, "Sweetheart, what can I do that would help you become a great man of God?" After a moment of contemplative silence, he replied, "When I come home from work, meet me at the door with no clothes on."

She was dumbfounded! Was he being silly or serious? She has since concluded that he was very serious.

Why not do something tonight that you *know* would truly please your mate?

3. *We need to fan the flames (or the flicker) of romance.* Barbara and I have a small table in our bedroom set with dishes for special evenings. (No, our bedroom isn't that big—it's just that crowded!) We put the kids to bed with books or let them watch a Walt Disney movie, and we share a candlelight dinner alone. We fan the flames by re-introducing ourselves, and talking.

What setting enables your love for your mate to spark or even ignite? Feed the flames—don't starve them.

4. *We need to have fun — but not at the expense of the other person.* Some of us are so serious about "the objective" that we've lost the fun of the relationship. Grins, giggles, and laughter ought to drift out of our bedrooms occasionally. (So what if the kids find out? It'll be good for them to know Mom and Dad have fun in bed!)

The Lord God who created 40,000 different kinds of butterflies never intended our physical intimacy to become boring. But some folks make it that way—especially by what they wear to bed. Men really aren't excluded here either, but I've had some men tell me privately they'd like to burn some of the burlap sacks their wives sleep in. Sure you may get cold—maybe you'll have to snuggle to stay warm! Snap out of the ruts. There are a lot of "classy" lingerie stores today—why not have fun shopping together? Christians ought to be their best customers. OUR GOD CREATED THE SEXUAL DIMENSION OF OUR LIVES!

5. *Add the element of surprise to your marriage bed.* Why not add some sizzle and creativity to your marriage bed? CAUTION: If the sexual area of your marriage has been a struggle, then it might be good to "ask permission" before cooking up something you think is wonderful, but may be offensive to your spouse (see Romans 15:1-7).

6. *Be patient with your mate.* Remember, the Christian life is the process of becoming like Christ. This area of married love and commitment demands that we be continually growing and learning about one another (see 1 Thessalonians 5:14-15).

7. *Beware of bitterness.* Perhaps nothing should be feared more than becoming resentful of your mate's sexual drive or "ap-

parent" lack of sexual appetite. Bitterness quenches the fires of romance. Keep short accounts and ask forgiveness when you fail or if you have become bitter (Ephesians 4:26-27). Make your relationship with your mate your priority.

Vonette Bright, wife of the president and founder of Campus Crusade for Christ, says this about sex: "It's just as important to be filled with the Holy Spirit in bed as it is in witnessing to another about Jesus Christ."

Why not turn out the lights early tonight?

12.

A License
to Build

*What would a godly marriage be worth
to the next ten generations?*

I was astounded recently by a full-page collection of advertisements that I read in Southern California's *Orange County Register* newspaper (read by about 800,000 adults daily). Under the heading "WEDDINGS & OCCASIONS," were listed thirty-eight categories of goods and services that related to getting married.

A casual glance revealed some fairly basic "necessities" for your average wedding: Cakes, Formal Wear, Flowers, Catering, Limousine Service (everything from a Rolls Royce to a White

Bentley), Chapel/Minister, etc. A careful reading, however, revealed more of our culture and its values. Some sections advertised bachelor/bachelorette parties, exotic dancers and all. One even boasted: "The best hunks and gorgeous ladies for your parties! Ask for Al." Also offered was a wedding planning seminar and a large firm selling "pre-marital agreements."

As I read that newspaper ad, I realized no one offered a service to help a couple overcome the problems that would arise in their marriage. Not one ounce of preventive education. Nothing.

"We don't need it," most couples would say. "We're already educated enough." And educated we are.

We study the latest data on new cars for weeks and months before buying one. Who would think of buying a personal computer without reading a few magazines and attending a seminar? Many of us spend sixteen years educating ourselves in how to make a living, yet how many of the courses really teach us how to live, how to make a good marriage or how to raise children?

Does it seem odd to you that, as a culture, we spend weeks training our dogs how to sit and heel, yet when it comes to marriage, we leave our children to fend for themselves?

Our athletes began training for the 1992 Olympics immediately following the 1988 Olympics in Seoul, Korea. What would have happened to the U.S. Hockey Team in the 1980 Olympics against Russia if they'd spent all their training, money, and energy on a big celebration *before* the event?

Marriage Prep 101?

Interesting, isn't it, that we spend so little time and money on preparation for marriage? It is said the average wedding costs at least $2,500, takes at least three months to plan and lasts about seventeen minutes. No wonder the marriages formed amid our twisted priorities often don't last as long as the engagement!

I'm not against nice weddings. I just attended a fantastic wedding in Houston. The difference, though, was that the couple spent a good deal of their time and money preparing for their marriage, not just for the wedding!

A close friend of mine once confessed, "It took me several years to realize a marriage license didn't make a marriage. It only gave me the right to begin building one."

What would a godly marriage be worth to the next ten generations? What kind of legacy could *one* godly marriage leave? We're so busy living for today that we are failing by the lasting standards of tomorrow and, most importantly, of eternity.

To fill a home with peace and stability, Proverbs teaches that three things are essential: knowledge, wisdom, and understanding (24:3-4). Not a single one was offered in that California newspaper's advertisement, at any price. But we don't have to follow the West Coast trends or *Bride* magazine's latest worldly advice.

Jesus Christ offers hope to a generation that has lost its moorings. His Word is the only source I really trust today when it comes to gaining knowledge, wisdom, and understanding. Especially where a lasting marriage relationship is concerned. The price of His wedding service? Free!

If you're burdened by these thoughts, why don't you tell your children what you have learned in your own marriage? Or better yet, go to your pastor and offer to start a pre-marriage course for couples who are getting married at your church. And remember, when it comes time for your son or daughter to marry, you can always require that they read the biblical blueprints for building a home before saying "I do!" You might just be helping them to build a legacy that lasts!

13.

Whatever Happened to the Family Tree?

It's been cut down by the ax of divorce.

An ax has fallen on the family tree. Having chopped off the branches and destroyed the fruit, the ax now cuts clean at the tree's trunk, leaving only the roots showing.

What is this destructive ax? Divorce. Far too many people use this destructive tool in trying to sever human problems from their lives.

Many who read this chapter have been the unwanted recipient of a heart-splitting divorce decree. I do not relish piercing their old wounds. Nor do I want to sound pious just because our marriage has worked when others' haven't. It is also not my intent to place a heavy yoke of guilt on another's neck.

But because so many of us have friends and relatives who are being tempted to divorce their mate, I've realized I cannot remain silent on this devastating issue.

The Tragedy of Divorce

There is no question that divorce brings deep humiliation and hurt. It can be seen on the faces of those who endure it. Newspapers print wedding pictures of smiling brides every week, but the divorce section contains only names. You can feel one man's anguish in a local classified advertisement:

> I want it known to the public that I made mistakes all through my marriage to Linda. I said things that weren't right. I battered and abused her both physically and verbally. I was unfair in the property settlement. I acted like a fool. I am lower than the ground I walk on. I have to live the rest of my life now without the person I truly love and who used to love me with no chance to undo the wrong I've committed. I lost the best thing that ever happened to me — my best friend. People, don't take your marriage for granted like I did. Divorce is not just a seven-letter word. I ask to be forgiven by all those concerned.

Over one million tragedies like that are taking place every year. We can no longer afford the luxury of being a spectator in this battle for the family. There is more at stake than just two isolated people when a couple chooses divorce. Our nation's future is literally on the line. How can our nation survive when a field full of stumps replaces its rich heritage of thriving family trees? The erosion of our most precious resource, our children, will have a devastating effect on our nation's future.

What Can We Do?

But there are a few solutions to the problem:

1. *We need to make certain our own marriages are divorce-proof.* Pastor/author Chuck Swindoll asks a great question: "Are

there any termites in your troth?" One of those termites could be complacency. Barbara and I wrote in our book about the need to compete continually for your mate. Even though the prize has already been won, you must continue to court your mate every day.

There is a formidable warning found in 1 Corinthians 10:12 to the one who thinks the tentacles of divorce can't reach into his marriage: "Let him who thinks he stands take heed lest he fall." How many ministers, missionaries and laymen have fallen into affairs and divorce after allowing romantic complacency to settle into their marriages?

2. *We need to resurrect the true meaning of commitment.* In this age of Lite beer, Lite fruit, and Lite syrup it's no wonder we exhibit "Lite Commitment." Our Lite vows are the reason why love these days is one-third less fulfilling.

A cartoon showed this marquee in front of a church:

THE LITE CHURCH
24% FEWER COMMITMENTS, HOME OF THE 7.5% TITHE,
5-MINUTE SERMONS, 15-MINUTE WORSHIP SERVICES.
WE ONLY HAVE 8 COMMANDMENTS—YOUR CHOICE.
WE USE JUST 3 SPIRITUAL LAWS,
AND WE HAVE AN 800-YEAR MILLENNIUM.
EVERYTHING YOU ALWAYS WANTED IN A CHURCH
. . . AND LESS!

That's what the world wants: More from less.

But commitment for a Christian is different. It's a sacred vow and promise to God. It's two people who hang in there for a lifetime during the best of times and the worst of times. It's two people who won't allow quitting to be a part of their vocabulary. It's a husband and wife who find working through problems much more rewarding than walking out.

And we need to pass on to our children the real definition of commitment while continually exposing the lies that their peers and the media propagate. A person who does not understand his ultimate accountability to God has little reason to fulfill a vow or commitment to another human being.

3. *We need to call Christians back to accountability.* I am nauseated by the growing number of Christians who advise their Christian friends to get a divorce. Upon hearing of the hurt and anguish of their friend, they don't reach for their Bible, but instead hastily grab a parachute and say, "Bail out!"

Yet even more in our ranks simply sit by, saying and doing nothing. They just let it happen. They ignore it. They've got the "Cain Syndrome" seen in Genesis 4:9; they continually ask, "Am I my brother's keeper?"

Hey, I understand. I've almost sweated blood with friends and family. It's pure anguish; I'd much prefer the high road of fun and pleasure. When there's only a slim thread of hope, what are you going to do?

You and I have got to go to the guy who just left his wife and three children. We've got to grab him by the shoulders and tell him it just isn't going to be that easy. He can't just walk out on them. And that woman in our Sunday school class? She can't leave her husband for this other guy and think things are going to be business as usual. Plead with them. Beg them. Pray with them. And get them some help. "'I hate divorce,' says the LORD, the God of Israel" (Malachi 2:16).

Please pray with me that God will purge our land of divorce. Pray for new laws that will make it more difficult for people to divorce. I am praying that the divorce rate will be cut in half by the year 2000. Will you join me?

14.

Rx: Laughter

Its medicinal properties lighten loads
and knit hearts together.

A Seattle teacher taught her third grade class the parts of the human body. All of the students passed her test except for one. When asked what the body was composed of, this sandy-haired, freckled-faced boy voiced his response: "The human body is composed of three parts: the brainium, borax, and abominable cavity. The brainium contains the brain. The borax contains the lungs, liver, and the living things. And the abominable cavity contains the bowels of which there are five—a, e, i, o, and u."

I chuckle every time I tell that story. Frankly, I like to laugh.

Someone has said that laughter is the sensation of feeling good all over and showing it in one place. Laughter releases chemicals in our bodies called endorphines, internal "drugs" that serve as pain killers. It's a legal tranquilizer that carries no side effects. I confess, I'm addicted to laughter.

Laughter is one of God's lubricants for life. Spiritual giants such as C. H. Spurgeon and Martin Luther were hooked on the stuff, too. Luther once kidded, "If they don't allow laughter in heaven, then I don't want to go there." He went on to add, "If the earth is fit for laughter then surely heaven is filled with it. Heaven is the birthplace of laughter." Spurgeon was once asked by the elders of his church to "tone down" his humor from the pulpit. The great English preacher replied, "If only you knew how much I held back, you would commend me."[1]

Some of the most fun-loving people I know are "spiritual giants" of our age. Bill and Vonette Bright enjoy laughing with each other and teasing one another as much as anyone I know. Chuck Swindoll has people who love his laugh almost as much as his preaching! Howard Hendricks peppers his messages with hilarious stories and some of the funniest faces you've ever seen. It doesn't take much to imagine that our Savior, Jesus Christ, had the most winsome smile and the heartiest laugh ever.

Serious Soreheads

But the way some Christians live, you'd think God had neglected to create a giggle-box. They act as though enjoying a couple of laughs a week is really excessive. They remind me of the sign I heard about located just outside the city limits of Aztec, New Mexico:

AZTEC, NEW MEXICO
5,667 FRIENDLY PEOPLE AND
6 OLD SOREHEADS

It's too bad that a Christian would fit into the "old sorehead" category.

The problem is that we take everything too seriously, as if

everything depends on *us*. Life can get heavy and burdensome, can't it? Sometimes, we're too busy to have fun. We become so goal-oriented that people, especially those in our family, get in the way of our task of living. Or we get worn down and cynical about the whole process.

Of course, life wasn't created by God to be friction-free, and laughter is not a panacea for a person's problems. Laughter doesn't level life's obstacles, but it does make the climb easier to bear.

When's the last time you got down on all fours and "ate" your child's tummy? Or wrestled him in the living room? How about the last time you did something really rowdy or goofy at the dinner table? How about a food fight? One evening we threw marshmallows at one another and laughed so hard we cried. Or how about reliving some funny memories with your family by looking at an old family photo album together? (After five years even the most professional wedding album is a guaranteed grin-getter.)

Long Live Laughter

Laughter and good marriages go well together. A Christian couple should sooner be found guilty of having too much laughter than of having too little. Too many marriages become a cemetery, not a celebration. Marriages in which couples stop courting (and having fun) die slowly of boredom. Fun lifts us out of the daily ruts and assassinates the drab, the boring, the dull, and the mundane. Laughter lightens loads and knits hearts together instantaneously.

Scripture recognizes the reality of laughter, "There is an appointed time for everything . . . A time to weep, and a time to laugh" (Ecclesiastes 3:1,4), and the medicinal qualities of laughter, "A merry heart doeth good like a medicine" (Proverbs 17:22).

God gave children a funny bone and giggle-box to balance all of those who are "overly intense." He gave our family kids who love to laugh, especially our daughter Rebecca. She lives to laugh. Her beaming smile and giggle is the all-time best. And when she gets going at the supper table, pandemonium breaks loose. Her giggle-box infects us all with an uncontrollable, delicious delight. In fact, we've renamed her because of her love for laughter: "Rebecca Jean Joy Susie-Q Rainey."

My family taught me how to laugh. I'll never forget my Dad's laugh (the best) and my Mom's sense of humor, which is still as sharp as ever. Some of my fondest memories are of laughing so hard the tears just streamed down our faces. I remember the time my Mom *gave herself* a Hoover vacuum cleaner for Christmas. She wrapped it and put it under the tree with this tag:

TO MY DEAR WIFE
FROM WARD

Our home was filled with practical jokes, many, like the vacuum cleaner, instigated by my mother. Teasing. Surprises. Laughter. It was a fun place to grow up; we all learned to laugh at ourselves and *with* one another.

Laughter in the Walls

Maybe at the end of your life you can experience what Bob Benson called "Laughter in the Walls":

> I pass a lot of houses on my way home—some pretty, some expensive, some inviting—but my heart always skips a beat when I turn down the road and see my house nestled against the hill.
>
> I guess I'm especially proud of the house and the way it looks because I drew the plans myself.
>
> It started out large enough for us—I even had a study—two teenage boys now reside in there. And it had a guest room—my girl and nine dolls are permanent guests. It had a room Peg had hoped would be her sewing room—the boys swinging on the Dutch door have claimed this room as their own.
>
> So it really doesn't look right now as if I'm much of an architect. But it will get larger again—one by one they will go away to work, to college, to service, to their own houses, and then there will be room—a guest room, a study, and a sewing room for just the two of us.
>
> But it won't be empty—every corner, every room, every

nick in the coffee table will be crowded with memories. Memories of picnics, parties, Christmases, bedside vigils, summers, fires, winters, going barefoot, leaving for vacation, cats, conversations, black eyes, graduations, first dates, ball games, arguments, washing dishes, bicycles, dogs, boat rides, getting home from vacation, meals, rabbits and a thousand other things that fill the lives of those who would raise five.

And Peg and I will sit quietly by the fire and listen to the laughter in the walls.[2]

Life is made up of pain. Disappointments. Pressure. Doubts. Trials. Confusion. We are all sapped of strength by these dark, ominous clouds. But, like an exploding shaft of sunlight in a dark room, laughter illuminates life by reminding us not to be so serious.

Why not leave a little laughter in the walls of your home tonight?

1. Charles Swindoll, *Growing Strong in the Seasons of Life* (Portland, OR: Multnomah, 1983).

2. Bob Benson, *Laughter in the Walls* (Nashville, TN: Impact Books, 1969).

15.

A
Wasted Day?

Plant the seeds of a cherished memory.

The Encyclopedia Britannica gives a half page to the accomplishments of the son of President John Quincy Adams, Charles Francis Adams. The younger Adams followed the political trail of his father and became a U.S. diplomat to Great Britain. The encyclopedia makes no mention of Charles' family, but Charles' diary does. An entry one day read: "Went fishing with my son today—a day wasted."

However another diary, that of his son Brook Adams, gives us a different perspective: "Went fishing with my father—the most wonderful day of my life."

Interesting, isn't it, how a little boy's perspective could be so different from his dad's?

But it's true of me, too. I can remember a fishing trip with Dad to Canada where I caught a trophy Northern Pike. And another outing to a local lake where he netted this small boy's catfish — a fish so small that it went through the holes in the net. He always kidded me about that fish. His laughter still echoes in my mind when I recall that skinny fish slipping *through* the net.

Childhood Memories, Cherished Possessions

It's interesting now as an adult how my mind can play tricks on me. Looking back, those days of vacation and moments of memories are among my most cherished possessions. Yet now that I'm grown, it seems that playing catch and going fishing are not nearly productive enough. No measurable goal is apparently achieved. Until, of course, I reflect on the value God places on a little boy or little girl.

I was reminded recently that not all men today have those memories of time with dad etched on the slate of their hearts. An associate of mine here in the Family Ministry recently wrote the following letter to his ministry partners, thanking them for their partnership in strengthening families. It speaks of memories of a different kind.

> I can still picture my dad bouncing me on his knee, coaching me in Little League, showing me how to shine my shoes, helping me reel in my first fish, and telling me stories about his early days as an undercover detective on the Berkley police force.
>
> I can still hear him saying the words, "Son, I love you." I can imagine him messing my hair, wrestling with me on the living room floor, and sharing a hot dog with me at a San Francisco Giants game.
>
> I can still see him puffing up his chest when he talked about me to his friends. He was proud to be my dad. He would do anything for me. I was *his* son; he was *my* dad. I was a chip off the old block.
>
> I can still see all this and much more, but I don't see it in the reservoir of fond memories. Instead, I recall it from an im-

agination and yearning that wished then and wishes now that it were so. My dad left home when I was three. I never really knew him.

When I drive home from the office, I'll often turn off the radio and in the quiet of the car I'll think about a little blond-headed, three-year-old somewhere who will grow up knowing his dad because *you* (my ministry partners) and *I* decided we wanted to make a difference.

I'm twenty-six years old. I still miss my dad (even though that's hard to admit). I even cry sometimes when I'm honest with myself about how I feel. Please pray for my dad. I don't believe he's met Jesus.

"I Never Really Knew Him"

The most piercing statement in my friend's letter is the words "I never really knew him." I couldn't help reflecting on the number of children today who will replay a similar record in their minds. No, not just those from broken homes, but those whose homes have a father and a mother in name only.

Some years ago at a Family Life Conference in Little Rock, a man came up, grabbed my hand and blurted out, "I became a father this weekend!" When I inquired further he said, "Oh no. My wife didn't have a baby; we already have three children. You see, I had 'fathered' three children, but I wasn't being a 'father' to them. This weekend I decided I was going to become a *real* father."

The little boy who went fishing with his dad, Brook Adams, lived most of his life as an agnostic, defying the roots of his Puritan ancestry. Near the end of his seventy-ninth year he returned to his home church, overcame his shyness and made a public profession of faith in Jesus Christ. I wonder if God used the memory of that fishing trip with his dad, linked with the spiritual values his father taught him, to bring Brook Adams to faith in Christ?

Take a kid fishing and teach him one spiritual truth. Just one memory. Just one truth. It may be the most memorable, "wonderful day" of his life.

16.

Teachable Moments

God sends those special moments along every day.
Are you seizing them?

Have you ever conducted a seminary course in a garage or convened a theology class in a sandbox? Have you ever held cathedral-like worship in your kids' hideout, or taught a Sunday school class in the kitchen while dinner was being prepared? I have. Each situation with our children represents a divinely ordered "teachable moment."

One morning I was pulling out of our garage on the way to the airport when my pre-teen daughter Ashley rushed out to give me just one more hug. I could tell something was troubling her.

Reaching out through the car window to hold her hand, I asked, "What's wrong, Princess?"

"I'm afraid your airplane is going to crash," she said, obviously a bit embarrassed by her admission. A recent airplane crash in Dallas had sent unsettling shock waves of fear through my daughter that were just now beginning to appear. It was one of those teachable moments, too valuable to squander by rushing off.

"Planes are safer than driving, Ashley," I attempted to assure her. "Besides, my life is in God's hands and He knows what He's doing."

By now my tender-hearted young Ashley was clutching my hand in both of hers and I could see that my theological lesson had fallen short of its mark. The pain of her fear was visible on her young face.

I went on: "Princess, fear is a normal emotion to experience for a young lady who is growing up. And what you need to learn is what to do with your fear once you experience it." Groping for the right words, I paused, then continued: "I won't always be here to answer your questions and concerns and to relieve all your fears. What I do need to do is share with you how to deal with your fears, how to take your fears to Jesus Christ. He's here right now, and He always will be." Gently, I added, "You're in the process of learning how to depend less on me and more on Him. He won't disappoint you.

"Ashley," I continued, "it's as if there are all these invisible electrical cords coming from you to me and your mom. And our responsibility as your parents is to unplug those cords from us and teach you how to plug them into God. We've got to continue the process of helping you become independent from us and dependent on Jesus Christ."

I then took one of her hands and gently "unplugged" one of those "invisible strands" from me. She frowned and then grinned as I guided her hand above her head and helped her visualize plugging into God. "Ashley," I said as I tenderly squeezed her hand, "I need to get to the airport, and you're going to have to take your fear to Jesus Christ. He can give you the peace."

"Impromptu Classes"

As I pulled out of the driveway, I waved at Ashley and she grinned back. My little girl was becoming a young lady. I thought about how the culture she is growing up in doesn't have many moorings, and how she would need to grow in her experience of depending on Christ.

A teachable child will attend one of these impromptu seminary classes—even in a garage at 7 A.M. Seizing the teachable moment means: (1) being constantly on the lookout for it, (2) taking the time to stop, (3) listening carefully to what's said (or not said), (4) gently sharing the truth, and (5) putting bookends of a loving relationship around your child as you teach him.

Not many days after my "garage encounter" with Ashley, I had the privilege of seizing another teachable moment with my ten-year-old son Benjamin.

It was evening and Barbara was away at a meeting. I had read a few stories to the kids, tucked them into bed, and prayed with them. I had told Benjamin that he could read until 9 o'clock and then "hit the hay." But at 9:05, as I was at work writing in my study, I felt a child's presence next to my chair. It was Benjamin.

Pushing my chair back from the computer and putting my arm around him, I said, "What's up, Buddy? You're supposed to be in bed, aren't you?"

Sheepishly, Benjamin replied, "Dad, I was up there reading *Huckleberry Finn* and there were these these robbers . . ." He paused, looking at the floor, then went on, "Dad, I'm afraid some robbers are going to come get me upstairs while I'm sleeping."

I pulled him close and gave him a firm hug and said, "Hey, it's all right. Let me tell you what happened with your sister Ashley the other morning." I went on to share about her fears and the process of unplugging her dependence on me and plugging it into God.

I had just taken Benjamin's hand to pull out one of those "invisible cords" and plug it in above his head into God, when I felt another child's presence in the room. It was Ashley. "What's going on?" she inquired.

"Benjamin is a little afraid," I responded. A big, sly grin broke across her face as Ashley realized her macho brother was scared. "Benjamin, you mean YOU are afraid?" Ashley said with surprise sprinkled with a tiny bit of glee.

"Yea," Benjamin responded, admitting he had a need. Ashley then went on to share from her garage theology class.

"It's Okay, Benjamin"

After praying with them, I scooted them off to bed. I turned and looked over my shoulder, watching them walk up the stairs together. They were side by side, and Ashley had her arm around her brother. "It's okay, Benjamin," she said, "I'm going through the same thing."

Teachable moments are opportunities for us as parents to imprint God's values on the next generation. They represent the God-ordained means by which we will pass on God's agenda to our children.

As a father, I realize that I must be "plugged in" to my heavenly Father if I am to impart real Christianity to my children, and if I am to spot and seize these God-ordered moments. He sends them to us everyday. Are you ready to seize them?

17.
Pebbles in
Your Sneakers

Can you give thanks for all the little irritations of life?

*I*t has been said that we are worn down less by the mountain we climb than by the grain of sand in our shoe. I agree. Would you like to know what pebbles seem to frequent my sneakers?

1. People who try to make me feel guilty.

2. My unbalanced checkbook.

3. My garage. (It continually proves the second law of thermodynamics—the universe is moving from order to disorder.)

4. The incessant ringing of the telephone.

5. Sibling rivalry.

6. Things that need fixing—a drippy faucet, a smoking fireplace, a leaky pipe in the ceiling, and more. Always more.

7. Car problems that always occur at the most inopportune times.

8. A whining child.

9. Things that aren't where I left them. (Or forgetting where I left them.)

10. More sibling rivalry.

11. An unresolved conflict with a family member.

12. And tripping over all the stuff that six children can drag out! I guess that is what has overwhelmed me recently. The floors at our place are symbolic of a lot of life's circumstances—piled with the unpredictable and regularly cluttered with chaos.

Assessing the Floor Debris

I took a census of our floors the other day. There were enough children's books on the floor to load a good-sized library truck. And Legos! Legos may spur creativity, but they drive me crazy. Ten zillion pieces specially designed to disappear forever down heat registers or to be sucked into the abyss of the vacuum cleaner.

I found enough dolls to populate Toy City. We have four daughters and more than twenty-five dolls (that's only a census estimate. No one knows for certain how many dolls really live here). The number of Cabbage Patch kids that sprinkled our floor made one think our floor was a garden.

In the dining room where we just finished dinner, the spilled food was enough to feed a small city. Plus an empty Coke can, two ribbons from some frazzled doll's hair and one coat. Our six-year-old threw it there hoping, I guess, that it would get lost amid the debris on the floor.

We have one child who is a pack-rat and another who, as a

miner, digs into everything the other is attempting to pack away. The result: more debris.

We don't live at the dump. It just looks that way, because it's the end of a very busy weekend that happens to be linked to a very busy month. Are we out of control? Partially, but doesn't it happen to everyone from time to time?

Little things. They get to us. Frequently.

I do know there are more serious problems in life, but today, tonight, right now, this is where I live. In the midst of the little things.

It's called reality. It reminds me of a bumper sticker I saw on a pickup truck some time ago: REALITY IS FOR THOSE WHO CAN'T COPE WITH DRUGS. I really do understand why we have a culture of cop-outs.

Does God Really Care?

Is God involved in the details of life? Could God possibly want to teach us something through a flat tire? Does He really want to invade every moment of our day, or would He prefer to reserve the 9:30-to-Noon slot on Sunday mornings?

One of the most practical spiritual truths in Scripture I've found is in 1 Thessalonians 5:18: "In everything give thanks." Just four little words that measure my walk with God. I'll never forget the first time I heard the concept of "giving thanks in all things." It was 100 percent foreign to me. I was accustomed to calling bad circumstances "bad luck," or getting ticked off, or just shrugging my shoulders while muttering, "What's the use?"

But I began to practice this new-found command, and to my amazement I started to notice a change in my attitude about life in general.

Do you believe God really wants us to give thanks in *all* things? "Isn't that a bit fanatical?" one might ask. "Why could this possibly be so important to God?" Let me suggest three reasons.

First, *giving thanks in all things expresses faith.* Faith in the God who knows what He's doing. Faith in the God who sovereignly rules in all that happens to us. Isn't that what He *wants* from us?

Second, *He commanded us to give thanks because He knew we wouldn't do it naturally.* Giving thanks in all things means I am no longer walking as a mere man, grumbling and griping, but walking as a spiritual man (1 Corinthians 2:14-15), a man who sees God at work even in the grains of sand that tend to fill my shoes.

Let's be honest: We'd rather gripe, complain, and be miserable about circumstances than give thanks.

And third, *He wants to teach us how to deal with the irritating grains of sand so we can get on with climbing the mountains He has set before us.* We have a tendency to feel the pebbles. And we think if we could just remove all those pebbles we could get on with living. But God wants to use those irritants to instruct us and help us "grow up." I wonder how many times He's had to teach me the same lesson before I finally learned it?

We Don't Really Have Problems

The following is an excerpt from a letter I wrote in 1976, and it contains a written snapshot of our family under the siege of circumstances.

> To start out with, we have been living out of suitcases for the past seven weeks, with our two little ones, both under two, going through Pampers like they owned the factory. You can guess what malady they were overtaken by!
>
> Our checks bounced because our paycheck was in the post office in Dallas, and we couldn't get it out to deposit it. All those rubbery checks were a stab to both my credit rating and my pride.
>
> My billfold and Barbara's purse were relieved from our presence (stolen or lost) in the big west Texas city of, get this, Rising Star.
>
> Not only did we lose all of our credit cards, but we also lost our identification. After a couple of hours of searching and

finding nothing, I was finally able to thank God that He was in control of our traveling disaster team.

Gluttons for punishment, we pressed on to Colorado where we decided to camp out with our two little ones (primarily because we didn't have enough capital to finance a motel room). That night a deluge of rain camped with us. Our tent was transformed from a shelter into a funnel. We were kept dry by massive barricades made of our two-year-old daughter's Pampers placed at strategic locations to soak up the minor floods which recurred in our tent.

By the time we finally arrived for Family Ministry training, we were wondering if we were really the ones the Lord wanted to use to start this ministry to the home. It seemed as though our home had quite a few bruises, scrapes, and lacerations. Let me confide in you that we had lost our perspective of thanking God "in all things."

Then a couple of days later a flash flood, the worst in Colorado history, hit Estes Park, taking the lives of seven fellow Campus Crusade for Christ staff members. Twenty-two wives of those in leadership barely escaped a twenty-foot wall of water by going up the side of the canyon in total darkness.

You know something? That disastrous incident really changed our perspective. We didn't really have any problems. God showed us that we had our lives and the privilege of serving the King of kings and the Lord of lords. God used that tragedy to teach us many valuable lessons.

Pressured? Overwhelmed? Why not consider giving thanks for that which is so weighty? Feeling hemmed in by life's daily drudgeries? Why not express faith and thankfulness that God knows what He's doing? Are you angry, resentful, and embittered about something over which you have no control? Why not give up these futile feelings and give thanks to the One who is in control? Had a bad day? Week? Month? Lift your eyes and heart by stopping right now and expressing "thanks" to the One who will not disappoint.

Do you have some grit and gravel in your shoe that feels like a quarry of boulders? Before you try to empty them out, why don't you stop right now and give thanks for that rock pile and ask Him to teach *you* what *you* might need to learn from it.

We never outgrow our need to re-learn one of the most fundamental tasks in the process of pulling weeds and planting seeds:

> *In everything give thanks;*
> *for this is God's will for you in Christ Jesus.*
> *1 Thessalonians 5:18*

18.

State of
the Union

*The state of our marriage union   determines
the strength of our nation.*

"The strength of a nation," said Abraham Lincoln, "lies in the homes of its people."

His observation is equally true today. The State of the Union is determined by the state of the marriage union, the condition of our nation's marriages, families, and homes.

What is the true condition of our country's homes today? By what yardstick can we accurately measure how our homes are doing? I would like to share with you an historical context that may bring goosebumps to the back of your neck.

After studying several of the greatest civilizations in the past, historian Carle Zimmerman wrote a book in 1947, *Family and Civilization*. In it he made several observations of the patterns he observed that led to the deterioration and the ultimate collapse of a civilization.

Historically Speaking

Zimmerman concluded that no society, nation or empire could survive the marked disintegration of its most basic unit — the family. He also found that, historically, the last stage of family destruction was marked by these developments.

1. Marriage lost its sacredness and was frequently broken by divorce.

2. Women lost their inclination for child-bearing and the birth rate decreased.

3. There was public disrespect for parents, parenthood, and authority in general.

4. There was an increase in juvenile delinquency, promiscuity, and rebellion.

5. There was a refusal of people with traditional marriages to accept family responsibilities.

6. There was an increasing desire for and acceptance of adultery.

7. There was an increasing desire for and spread of sexual perversions of all kinds, including homosexuality.

Writing almost forty years ago, Zimmerman concluded that America, viewed against the plumbline of past cultures, was already experiencing the final stage in the breakdown of families and nearing a collapse.

A Prophecy Fulfilled

Think about Zimmerman's study as you look at the state of our country today.

1. *Divorce* — half of all new marriages now end in divorce.

2. *Child-bearing* — in 1984, there were approximately 1.5 million abortions in the United States, and over the past twenty years the birth rate has declined 32 percent.

3. *Respect for authority* — between 1977 and 1983 there was a 53 percent increase in the number of assaults on public school teachers.

4. *Juvenile delinquency and promiscuity* — today, one-third of all crimes involve teenagers; there are more than two million teenage runaways and over 600,000 teenage prostitutes.

5. *Family irresponsibility* — of the two million runaways, approximately 560,000 represent children who have been deserted by their parents.

6. *Adultery* — recent statistics indicate that as many as two out of three husbands and one out of two wives have been unfaithful at some time during their marriage.

7. *Sexual perversion* — today it is estimated that as many as five percent of Americans may be homosexuals. This year 250,000 children will be sexually abused in their homes.

Why is this happening? Because the State of the Union is determined by the state of the marriage union.

What can we do? We read in the Bible that when Nehemiah learned that the walls of Jerusalem lay in ruin, he immediately wept, fasted, and prayed (Nehemiah 1). For four months he prayed. Four months!

Then he acted. After months of prayer, he had a plan that was etched on his heart and mind by the hand of God. Nehemiah saw the walls of Jerusalem rebuilt in fifty-five days. Even his enemies stood in disbelief at the achievement. God intervened and brought order, cooperation and action out of what had been chaos for near-ly ninety years.

A Prayer for Deliverance

America today is much like Jerusalem then. Our nation's wall, its national security — the family — lies in ruins and is in desperate need of being rebuilt. As in Nehemiah's time, the task before us needs God's intervention as never before. We desperately need God's deliverance for the Christian family. We need to pray that:

1. Christian marriages and families will exemplify the love of God to a world that is perishing.

2. We in the church will have wisdom and courage in standing against divorce and the impact it is having on our families, while having compassion and love for those who suffer its devastation.

3. Our children will marry wisely.

4. The legacy we leave our children will not be one of materialism and spiritual apathy, but of caring concern for a world that needs to know Jesus Christ as Lord and Savior.

5. God will bring the resources (money, talent, leadership, technology, and manpower) to all who are striving to strengthen families.

Let's pray for the State of the Union by praying for the state of the marriage union:

> God, come and rebuild the wall. Come and repair all the broken pieces of our families today. Confuse our enemies, O Lord, and weaken their influence for evil. And above all may Jesus Christ be Lord in every Christian home, to Your glory. Amen.

P·A·R·T · T·W·O

Pulling Weeds, Planting Seeds

In My World

19.

An Affair of the Heart

*How do we respond to God in the best of times,
and in the worst of times?*

To begin his classic novel, *A Tale of Two Cities,* Charles Dickens penned the immortal words: "It was the best of times, it was the worst of times."

Was Dickens indulging in an overstated contradiction? Hardly. Life is both sweet and sour . . . simultaneously. It has been said, "Life is like licking honey off a thorn."

Sometime ago I was tasting the "sweet" savor of a great year for the Family Ministry. Our conferences had been growing rapidly. The best of times.

At about the same time I was also stretched thin by the adversary. Pressure. Attacks. Seemingly insurmountable problems. Even a sleepless night or two, a real rarity for me. The worst of times.

Then, as Barbara and I were beginning to get our strength back after this grueling stretch, we found out she was pregnant ...again...and not planned, at least not by us. It would mean that, in God's sovereign and loving will, we'd have six children ages ten and under. The best of times?

The Day Our Plans Changed

A couple months later God *really* got our attention. It started out quite normal. A busy, noisy breakfast. Beds to be made. Kids to be dressed. Hair to be combed. We had loads of plans for that day. *Our* plans.

But His plan was different. Barbara walked into our bedroom and fell on the bed complaining that her heart was beating fast. It had happened before. Seven years ago her heart raced at close to three hundred beats per minute for more than seven hours, and it nearly claimed her life. We knew it could happen again. And now it *was* happening, only this time she was three months pregnant.

As we rushed to the hospital, a hundred thoughts flashed across my mind. Praying for Barbara, I wondered how quickly the doctors would be able to slow her heart. Would I soon be saying good-bye to the woman I loved, and be left alone to raise five children?

Are these the worst of times? NO! Not for a Christian. For even death—the selfish, cursed enemy of man—has been "swallowed up in victory" (1 Corinthians 15:54-58). Even tribulations, the Scriptures tell us, produce hope (Romans 5:3-5). *But I don't like this way of producing hope,* I thought as our van rounded the corner to the hospital. *We don't* need *this right now.*

There the doctor went to work while Christians across the

country prayed. Barbara got sicker. Her heart beat so fast, it was not filling up with blood, causing her to experience low blood pressure. This low blood pressure could harm the baby if it continued.

The doctor made a quick decision. Using electric shock, he successfully reduced her heart rate to seventy-five beats per minute.

Afterward, through tears, we gave thanks for God's intervention. The baby's heart was fine, ticking along at a normal 152 beats per minute. Barbara, also, was okay.

Barbara and I talked quite a bit after that terrifying event. We *think* we are in control. We think we can *plan* our lives. We struggle over so many insignificant things. What *really* matters? we found ourselves asking.

Vanity of Vanities

In the midst of these best and worst of times, a certain book reached us like a beacon in the darkness. It's a book that rips away the veil of idealism about life. It deals with our pursuit of life, purpose and significance. It gives meaning to life's storms, to prosperity, to riches, to our search for security.

The book? Ecclesiastes.

In its pages Solomon paints the paradoxes of life better than Charles Dickens ever dreamed. He writes that, whether we're experiencing the best or worst of times, God must be our reference point for life. If not . . . then life is vanity. Emptiness. Void of meaning. In short, a failure.

As I drove away from the hospital later that afternoon, I reflected on how different people respond to crisis situations. And I wondered, *What is their reference point for a life and death situation? Where is the meaning of it all?*

That night as I put our five children to bed, we crowded together and prayed. Benjamin, our eight-year-old, prayed as only a child can: "Father, we give thanks that Mommy got sick cause we know you want us to give thanks in everything . . . and we give thanks that's she's okay, too."

He prayed with childlike faith, and a mature perspective! He understands how God wants us to respond in the best of times, *and* in the worst of times. Character is to be built at *all* times.

20.
No
Magic Wands

When my will clashes with God's, will I trust
He really does know what's best for me?

(Barbara's perspective of the same event.)

*T*hough we wish it were so at times, life is not a fairy tale. God
is not a fairy godmother with a magic wand whisking our
troubles away. He has plans and purposes for our lives far greater
than fairy magic. The problem for me is the clash between two purposes and wills: God's and mine.

Several years ago, I experienced a particularly memorable conflict between God's will and plan, and my own. Unlike Cinderella, I found no magic wand wishing away my troubles.

Tuesday morning dawned clear and warm with the promise of another hot July afternoon to follow. We proceeded with our normal routine of dressing and helping children dress, eating breakfast and looking for lost tennis shoes. A couple of hours later while driving home after dropping the children off at their summer activities, I suddenly became dizzy, almost blacking out. Though I could hardly see, I managed to pull into a parking space. Dropping my head on the steering wheel, I prayed, "Lord, please let me get home." I was only a block away. My vision cleared, and I slowly drove home.

My next prayer as I parked the car was that Dennis, who was working at home when I left, would still be there. Dropping my purse and keys on the kitchen floor, I made my way to the bedroom and fell on the bed, greatly relieved that my second prayer was answered: Dennis was home. After a couple of quick phone calls, he helped me back to the car.

The Race Is On

My heart raced at two hundred to three hundred beats per minute while we raced to the hospital. My mind was racing, too: *Why was it happening again? Why now? How long would it last this time?* It had been seven years since we'd discovered this congenital heart problem.

Three months before, I had discovered another plan God had for my life that was not my own. We were nearing the end of an unusually busy spring, one that contained more than its share of pressure. We were longing for summer and a break in the action.

During those months I felt particularly stretched with our five active children. I'd always wanted a large family, and I was grateful for each of those five treasures; still, I was glad to be finished with pregnancies and babies, and was looking forward to graduating from nursery duty.

The days were warming up and the flowers in our small garden began to branch out and bloom. I planned to do some painting on our deck and wicker chairs before the real heat of summer arrived. Suddenly my motivation disappeared. I forgot about the flowers and the beautiful spring days.

I was pregnant. Again. The news of this pregnancy caught me completely off guard.

What Does He Think He's Doing?

Didn't God know I had all I could handle? Didn't He know I didn't want to go through this again? I was sick physically, drained mentally, and tired from just thinking about six children. I acknowledged my submission to God's will for my life, and told Him I would obey and follow, but it took a longer than usual time for my feelings to catch up.

During the next two months, I prayed and cried and read Scripture, falling asleep in the middle of verses. Life was reduced to whatever took the least amount of effort. Discouragement and feelings of inadequacy often took over my emotions. I continued to wonder why, and to wonder how I could do what God had called me to do.

During this time of adjusting to God's will, I listened one day to a story on cassette tape with my children. It was about Glenn Cunningham, a track star of the 1930s who had overcome a doctor's prediction when he was nine years old that he'd never walk again. This young boy clung to a verse his father had read to him. It was Isaiah 40:31.

I got out my Bible as soon as I could and read the verse in Isaiah 40 and into Isaiah 41. I stopped at verse 10, which says: "Fear not, for I am with you, be not dismayed for I am your God; I will strengthen you, I will help you, I will uphold you with my victorious right hand."

I reread it several times. It encouraged me to remember that He who had called me to be a mother and who had chosen to give me this new child would not only be with me, but would also give me the strength and help I needed.

Now it was Tuesday, July 3. I lay in the coronary intensive care unit. My heart was out of control. But my main concern was for the child within me. Knowing that God can heal and protect, but also that He is the giver and taker of life, I prayed simply that He would protect our baby and spare its life and mine. I continued that prayer and committed my life into His hands as I lay there growing weaker and weaker, only semiconsciously aware of the flurry of activity around my bed.

After two hours of trying different medications, I was put to sleep and my heart was re-timed using electric shock treatment. When I woke, the nurse told me I was okay and that the baby's heartbeat was a strong 152 beats per minute. I was so relieved I cried for joy.

Listening to God's Voice Takes Time

Through this pregnancy and hospitalization I once again learned that accepting God's will for my life is often a difficult assignment. God's will requires adjustment. It also may carry a price tag called suffering, whether it be emotional, mental, or physical. One thing, however, is certain about God's will. Romans 12:2 tells us His will is good, acceptable, and perfect. God doesn't make mistakes. I am being conformed to the image of Christ. One day that will be completed in an instant and, from our human perspective, as if by magic.

But for now God has chosen to conform us, not by magic, but through a process called walking by faith. A quick glance at Hebrews 11 tells us faith requires not a feeling, but obedience to the truth: right choices, trust in a sovereign God, and looking ahead to the future to which He has called us.

God's will in each of our lives is much like a quilt. An overall pattern or design is made up of hundreds of pieces. Some pieces are large, some small, some pale, some brightly colored. Choosing to be conformed to Christ's image will require pieces in our lives that, when viewed up close and apart from the whole, seem difficult, unpleasant, and dark. But God views the whole pattern as He works His will in our lives.

My part as I view the pieces one at a time is to remember that He is the Creative Designer. With this knowledge, I choose to trust His plan, knowing that His grace gives me time to conform to His will when the pieces I see are not of my choosing.

Six months later Laura Victoria Rainey was born on a cold January night. She's quite healthy and normal, unaffected by my racing heart episode and all the medications and treatments she endured with me while still in the womb. She has added joy and smiles to our family and to my life.

God Knows Best

Looking back on those days, I see that I learned some lessons that only experience can teach. One is a greater appreciation of God's sovereignty and a greater willingness to follow *His* plan for my life.

Second, I learned that God will enable me to do what He has planned for me. "Faithful is He who calls you and He will also bring it to pass" (1 Thessalonians 5:24).

I also realized, though I confess I've not yet mastered this knowledge, that as a Christian I often forget I am human. I expect of myself instant maturity. I don't consciously think of Christianity as a fairy-tale life, like Cinderella's, but in my finite ability to understand and perceive reality, I'd rather live in the magic wand world. I would love a "Bibbidy Bobbidy Boo" formula of escape when life gets tough.

I'm thankful for these lessons I've experienced as a result of God's interventions in my life. Difficulties afford me the opportunity to know Him better and become more conformed to Christ.

The question I asked myself that summer I now will ask you, for you too may find yourself in the middle of circumstances that are not your design, but God's: "What difference will this portion of God's will make in my life? Will I resist and insist on my own plan, or will I submit and allow God to further conform me to His image?"

The choice is yours, and mine.

21.
For
Goodness' Sake

Pulling the weed of disobedience.

Our children continue to teach us about being good. Sure, we train them, but occasionally (without knowing it) they'll take us to school. One day our eight-year-old, Samuel, typed out a treatise titled: "HOW TO BE GOOD." The following is Samuel's own, unedited work shared with the permission of the "budding" author for your benefit:

HOW TO BE GOOD

1. Obay you parntes and GOD.

2. Do want other kids want to do.

3. Do not be selfish.

4. Be good to babbysearts.

5. Do want parntes say.

6. Do not cheat.

7. Play right.

8. Be a good player.

9. Dont be a por sport.

10. Do not cuse.

Not bad, huh? Who knows what triggered this active boy to etch out his inspired list. Barbara and I pulled Samuel aside and complimented him on his ten tips on "How To Be Good." He shrugged his shoulders and responded with a bashful grin, "Yea, I guess it's okay."

God Defines Goodness

Samuel's conclusions are a child's perception of several of the Ten Commandments. I wonder how many of us could even name all the Ten Commandments. Why not pull out Exodus 20 and read and discuss them at dinner tonight? I'll give you a head start with a quick look at four of them that tell us how to be good.

1. You shall have no other gods before me.

I'm certainly convinced that one of modern Christianity's worst forms of idolatry is our worship of things. Materialism. Barbara and I constantly struggle to stay out of this quicksand. We don't want to leave a legacy of materialism for our kids. (By the way, this is the one commandment to which God attaches a warning that He will visit our sins on our children—even to the third and fourth generation.)

Another form of idolatry is our worship of self-fulfillment. Careers, the number of children we decide to have, our attitude about divorce, and our general preoccupation with "what's in it for me" have all been sired by the personal rights movement. Russian dissident Aleksandr Solzhenitsyn said it best: "The time has come to speak not so much about human rights, but about our human responsibilities."

2. *You shall not take the name of the Lord your God in vain.*

Taking God's name in vain is more than just using His name as a swear word. It means "to take His name to mean nothing." "Praise the Lord" can become slang if we say it only out of habit. God is holy and sacred, the God to be feared. If we are to have a "good" family, then its members must hold His name in highest respect.

3. *You shall not commit adultery.*

I was stunned by a recent poll in one of our local newspapers. The question asked was, "Would you cheat on your spouse (have an affair) if you knew you would not get caught?" How do you think the "good" people of Arkansas, people who live just a few miles from the buckle of the Bible Belt, answered that question? *Seventy-four* percent said they would cheat! I immediately wondered what the national response would be: 80, 85, maybe 90 percent?

We need a moral epidemic of "good" teenagers, as well as adults. How about talking about the value of virginity and fidelity with your pre-teens or teenagers at the dinner table tonight? Or preparing your first- or second-grader for all they're hearing or going to hear about sex at school?

4. *You shall not steal.*

A good businessman or businesswoman obeys God in his dealings with his employer, employees and clients. He reports all of his income at income tax time. Why would a Christian who wants to be "good" have a radar detector that warns a driver when police are checking for speeders?

Are you a "good" employee, putting in a string of hard-working hours toward a hard day's work? Or are you an average employee, who fudges on expense reports (but not as much as "all the others"), works maybe three-fourths of the time, and fosters a critical attitude toward those in authority by picking away at their flaws and magnifying their failures?

We know that these commandments (and the other six not mentioned) contain a moral snapshot of God's character and His goodness. We find out what He's like and how we are to live by looking at these sacred laws and by living them.

The Obedience Struggle

But even though these commandments make sense, why do we struggle with obedience to God?

The prophet Isaiah says it best: "All we like sheep have gone astray; each of us has turned to his own way . . . " (53:6). In short, we have a will that is contrary to God's will. We resist Him and rebel against His commandments. As a result, we get exactly what we wanted: our own way.

Yet sheep are not the only creatures that resemble man's self-ish plight. Dogs do, too. I can see my response to God especially mirrored in the training of that special breed of bird dogs known as retrievers. Chesapeake Bay retrievers, black Labradors, and golden retrievers must all be trained to fetch and return to their masters.

Each special breed of dog, however, responds to this training differently. The Chesapeake Bay retriever is one of the strongest-willed. Trainers must use a club to teach this "hard-headed hound" to obey the commands of his master. Lighter training materials are used on a black Labrador; only the sting of a freshly cut switch is needed to teach him to follow. But the golden retriever is the most sensitive of all; the trainer needs only his voice to train him. Evidently, his "heart" is tender to the tone of the master's voice.

Like those pure-bred retrievers, we respond to our Master's training in different ways. Perhaps all you need to do is hear a whisper of displeasure in your Master's voice, and you'll correct a bad attitude. Others may need the switch or even the club. Ouch! Which retriever are you most like? (Not unlike their parents, our children have different natures resulting in different responses to training. As parents we need to adapt our "training style" so that we don't crush one child or be too lenient with another.)

So what does it mean to be good? It means that we are to be like the God we represent. It means we are not called to be merely "above average" in our ethics, but pure and as good as God. It means we need to be honest when no one is looking, when only our children are watching, and when our neighbors or associates tempt us to be bad.

We need good Christians who are determined to establish good Christian homes. We need a resurgence of good homes, families who are committed to obeying God.

Tocqueville said it best: "America is great because America is good. When America ceases to be good, she will cease to be great." Good homes will preserve our nation from moral collapse in this generation and the next. What about your home?

22.

A Life of No Regrets

Pulling the weed of bitterness from our lives.

S ports broadcaster Bill Stern shocked historians when he revealed that Abraham Lincoln's last earthly thoughts and utterances were about baseball.

Stern reported that as Lincoln lay dying in a hotel across the street from the Ford Theatre, he allegedly roused from his coma and demanded that General Abner Doubleday be summoned to his bedside. In haste Doubleday arrived at the President's side to hear Lincoln's last directive and words: "General, you must keep baseball alive. America will need it in the trying days ahead." Then he died.

Believe it or not.

The surprising last words of another great man are recorded as a lesson for us in 1 Kings 2:8-9. King David gives his final directive to the new king, his son Solomon:

> And behold, there is with you Shimei the son of Gera the Benjamite, of Bahurim; now it was he who cursed me with a violent curse on the day I went to Mahanaim. But when he came down to me at the Jordan, *I swore to him by the Lord, saying, "I will not put you to death with the sword." Now therefore, do not let him go unpunished,* for you are a wise man; and you will bring his grey hair down to Sheol (hell) with blood.

The next verse reads, "Then David slept (died) and was buried."

David: A Gangster?

Here a man of God talks like a dying gangster putting out a contract on a guy's life. Why were David's last words vengeful? Why did he go back on a vow? To find out, we need to go back to the actual event described in 2 Samuel 16:5-14.

David's life in those troublesome days was in decline. The sins of his adultery with Bathsheba and his murder of her husband hung like a thick, suffocating fog around him. Additionally, one of David's sons, Absalom, was attempting to overthrow his rule.

David was on his way out of Jerusalem in total disgrace. Further humiliation haunted him as Shimei threw rocks and dirt at David, cursing him and accusing him of evil.

David's response to Shimei was one of *apparent* trust in God. David told those who were with him to leave Shimei alone, that God was behind the man's actions. David's words seemed to drip with "spiritual perspective" as he stated his belief in God's sovereign control and his hope that God would perhaps bless him for his kind response to Shimei.

The drama continues, however, when a few days later we find loose-lipped Shimei hurrying to David's camp (2 Samuel 19:16-23).

He had come to his senses and realized that to curse the king meant death. Finding David, Shimei quickly sputtered a confession of guilt and asked for clemency.

David's promise was clear: "You shall not die." Case closed, right? Wrong!

What happened to David between that event and his deathbed plot for revenge? Though we won't find it in the Bible, it doesn't take a doctorate from Jerusalem University to realize that David finally gave in to resentment. Thus his last words reveal him as a man who died embittered against another.

Bitterness: The Corrosion of a Heart

Do you know any people like that? Filled to the brim with resentment and bitterness? Enslaved to a critical attitude about everyone and everything? How many times have you walked away from such a person and silently prayed, "Please, Lord, don't allow me to become like that person"?

People don't *become* bitter overnight. Bitterness comes as a result of choices—many wrong choices. Like pouring battery acid over your heart, these corroding attitudes eat away internally over a lifetime.

When we choose to forgive, we choose to give up the right of punishment. Forgiving someone doesn't necessarily mean we forget immediately or even completely, but it does mean we no longer hold a private grudge that desires to punish.

Someone has said that a grudge gets heavier the longer we carry it. That explains why many old people die as David did—weighed down, heavy with bitterness.

The way we live and handle our relationships today will determine our countenance and attitude when we are in our sixties, seventies and eighties. David didn't *become* bitter on his deathbed. He *allowed* its seed to sprout and flourish in the garden of his mind over many years.

So, what can we do to keep from harboring angry or vengeful

feelings? Let me recommend three important steps that I've learned.

1. *Cut down any bitterness growing in your life and dig it up, roots and all.*

Hebrews 12:15 warns us to not let a "root of bitterness spring up" in our lives. A root grows from a germinated seed that has been nourished and cultivated. Dig up those bitter roots and eradicate them from your life by confessing them one by one to God (see 1 John 1:5-10). God promises forgiveness to all who confess their sin.

After restoring your relationship with God, it may be appropriate to also go to the person you have been angry with and seek his or her forgiveness.

2. *Choose your inner occupation and career path: judge or forgiver.*

"Let all bitterness and wrath and anger and clamor and slander be put away from you, along with all malice. And be kind to one another, tenderhearted, forgiving each other, just as God in Christ also has forgiven you" (Ephesians 4:31-32).

Pursuing the occupation of judge by punishing another with resentment, bitterness or anger for the hurt you have suffered will boomerang on you. Baseball player Satchel Paige said it well: "What goes around, comes around."

Forgiveness, on the other hand, says, "I will give up my right to punish you for how you have wronged me."

Take no chances. Rid yourself of the acidic residue of anger and join the "Seventy Times Seven Club." Christ said we are to forgive one another seventy times seven (Matthew 18:22). His point was that we must forgive others as the Father forgives us: over and over again.

Who knows? Maybe when you retire you'll be known as a compassionate forgiver of others and not as a critical judge.

3. *Experience peace by resolving conflicts as they occur.*

"Be angry, and yet to not sin; do not let the sun go down on your anger, and do not give the evil one an opportunity [literally, 'don't give him a foothold']" (Ephesians 4:26-27). No one really enjoys harboring a poisonous grudge against another, but many times our pride keeps us from going to others and confessing our error. Think of it. Which would you rather deal with: the short-term, emotional pain of asking another to forgive you for your anger, *or* carrying the bitter, cancerous feelings for a lifetime?

We are commanded to "pursue peace with all men" (Hebrews 12:14). Look at this practical approach to relationships found in Romans 12:17-21: "Never pay back evil for evil to anyone . . . If possible, so far as it depends on you, be at peace with all men. Never take your own revenge . . . Do not be overcome by evil, but overcome evil with good."

Satisfied With Life?

Twenty years from now you *will be* the person you are *choosing to become* today. Are you choosing to pull weeds of bitterness out of your life and plant seeds of forgiveness?

It is my hope to live and die not as David did, but as the Old Testament patriarch Abraham did a thousand years earlier: "Abraham breathed his last and died in a ripe old age, an old man and *satisfied with life*" (Genesis 25:8).

23.

Pressure With
a Purpose

Pulling the weed of stress.

*D*oes pressure ever get to you? It gets to me. Let me share a slice of our lives I recorded in my journal several years ago:

A plumber has just informed me our house could explode any minute because of a faulty gas line. A corner of the wallpaper is peeling above the shower. On the way to the office I hit every red light possible and arrived late. As I entered my office, an associate informed me of two urgent situations needing immediate decisions. A three-inch pile of unanswered letters on my desk cries out for immediate attention. PRESSURE. Barbara is on the phone needing a decision from me on refinishing our ancient hardwood floors: "What color of stain should we use? When should the floor man come? Should we do the kids' closet? Who's going to move the couch? Remember it's the one that has a queen size hide-a-bed in it."

And if that weren't enough, all six of us were leaving in twenty-four hours, after being on the road for eight weeks, to speak at a Family Camp in California.

That day, Barbara started sneezing. Ashley and Samuel chorused in, and by midnight half of the Rainey Zoo suffered from asthma. In less than eight hours we were to leave for Family Camp. Who needs Family Camp? We prayed about canceling. The next morning the lawn still needed mowing, the kids were still sick and Rebecca was crying for Cheerios. I had to get this tribe to the airport, but our bills were due and the paycheck hadn't come. The phone rang as we locked the door, but we had to ignore it or miss our plane. The kids chimed in unison, "Could you stop for doughnuts, Daddy?" Secretly I thought, *Who needs Family Camp, hardwood floors, or DOUGHNUTS? This must be a sinister plot to overthrow my family!*

The Sinister Plot of Stress

As I reflect back on those pressure-packed moments of the summer of '81, I think life was pretty simple then compared to today. Stress, it seems, has become the ninth member of our family. My hope is that God is using stress to transform us all into diamonds. I've heard it said that diamonds are just lumps of coal that have been under pressure for a long time. And there are times when I feel like a load of coal!

How do we live with pressure? Is pressure always bad?

J. Hudson Taylor, the great pioneer missionary to China, gave some great advice: "It matters not *how great* the pressure is, only *where* the pressure lies. If we make sure it never comes *between* us and our Lord, then the greater the pressure, the more it presses us *to Him.*"

But sometimes I want out. Don't you? We often think less

stress would be better (and sometimes that's true). But many of us want less pressure from the things that are good for us to bear. There *can* be positive effects from pressure. It's not pressure, but our *response* to pressure, that determines pressure's effect on us. The late Joe Bayly, a modern-day psalmist, captures what our response should be in his poem, "A Psalm While Packing Books":

This cardboard box
Lord
See it says
Bursting limit
200 lbs. per square inch.
The box maker knew
how much strain
the box would take
what weight
would crush it.
You are wiser
than the box maker
Maker of my spirit
my mind
my body.
Does the box know
when pressure increases close to
the limit?
No
it knows nothing.
But I know
when my breaking point
is near
And so I pray
Maker of my soul
Determiner of the pressure
within
upon
me
Stop it
lest I be broken
or else
change the pressure rating

> of this fragile container
> of Your grace
> so that I may bear more.[1]

Isn't that what we need to ask God for? Our prayer should be, "Change the pressure rating and broaden my shoulders. Strengthen me, O Lord, to handle that which has come into my life." He will. He promised. Here is His response to that prayer:

> Come unto me, all who are weary and heavy laden, and
> I will give you rest. Take My yoke upon you, and learn from Me,
> for I am gentle and humble in heart; and you shall find rest for
> your souls. For My yoke is easy and My load is light" (Matthew
> 11:28-30).

Only Jesus can promise that. Only Jesus can truly deliver rest from stress.

So then, how must we learn to view stress in our lives? Perhaps the burdens we desire to "cast off" are those that God wants to use in our lives to press us to Him and to cause us to trust Him. Totally. Completely. Without reservation.

Some Burdens Are Worth Bearing

The following parable of Sadhu Sundar Singh, a Hindu convert to Christianity, beautifully illustrates how God wants to use burdens and heavy pressures in our lives.

Shortly after coming to Christ, Sadhu felt called to become a missionary to India. Late one afternoon Sadhu was traveling on foot through the Himalayas with a Buddhist monk. It was bitterly cold and the wind felt like sharp blades slicing into Sadhu's skin. Night was fast approaching when the monk warned Sadhu that they were in danger of freezing to death if they did not reach the monastery before darkness fell.

Just as they were traversing a narrow path above a steep precipice, they heard a cry for help. Down the cliff lay a man, fallen and badly hurt. The monk looked at Sadhu and said, "Do not stop. God has brought this man to his fate. He must work it out for himself." Then he quickly added while walking on, "Let us hurry on before we, too, perish."

But Sadhu replied, "God has sent me here to help my brother. I cannot abandon him."

The monk continued trudging off through the whirling snow, while the missionary clambered down the steep embankment. The man's leg was broken and he could not walk. So Sadhu took his blanket, made a sling of it, and tied the man on his back. Then, bending under his burden, he began a body-torturing climb. By the time he reached the narrow path again, he was drenched in perspiration.

Doggedly, he made his way through the deepening snow and darkness. It was all he could do to follow the path. But he persevered, though faint with fatigue and overheated from exertion. Finally, he saw ahead the lights of the monastery.

Then, for the first time, Sadhu stumbled and nearly fell. But not from weakness. He had stumbled over an object lying in the snow-covered road. Slowly he bent down on one knee and brushed the snow off the object. It was the body of the monk, frozen to death.

Years later a disciple of Sadhu's asked him, "What is life's most difficult task?"

Without hesitation Sadhu replied: *"To have no burden to carry."*

May the burdens you and your mate carry press your hearts to Christ and merge you into one as you rightly respond to circumstances together. Tonight before retiring, why not spend a few moments in prayer together. As a couple, take those "things" that are pressuring you to the One whose burden is easy and whose yoke is light.

1. Joseph Bayly, *Psalms of My Life* (Wheaton, IL: Tyndale House Publishers, 1969).

24.
Divine
Appointments

You really wouldn't want to miss a single one.

A divine appointment is a meeting with another person that has been specifically and unmistakably ordered by God.

Have you ever had a divine appointment? I have. I sometimes wonder how many of these supernaturally-scheduled meetings I've missed because I didn't have my spiritual radar turned on.

The Scriptures say, "The steps of a man are established by the Lord" (Psalm 37:23). After nearly twenty years of walking (off and on, but mostly on) with God, I can tell you that watching God set up these appointments is a thrill beyond comparison.

One of my friends and associates in the Family Ministry, Bill Howard, experienced one such heavenly appointment, and his account appears below. It all began with a routine trip one April to promote the Family Life Conference in San Antonio, Texas.

As I was waiting for my plane, I noticed a man in his mid-twenties dressed in a red warm-up suit. He stood out because he was severely disfigured, an obvious victim of fire. I recall feeling compassion accompanied with a slight feeling of repulsion because of his grotesque appearance.

Little did I know that a friend was praying that I would have the opportunity to share Christ with someone on the plane that day. So, like the conductor of a symphony, God began to orchestrate circumstances to accomplish His purposes.

As we boarded the plane it became apparent that it was going to be a packed flight. A little annoyed, I arrived at my seat only to find that another man with a similar name had taken my seat. As I stood in the aisle and waited for the attendant to assign me another seat, I noticed that the disfigured man in the red warm-up suite had the same lot as me. I felt uncomfortable for him as I watched people stare at his abnormal appearance. After all the other passengers were seated there were only two seats left on the entire plane . . . together . . . in row seven.

Here I was, sitting next to the very man at whom everyone had stared.

As the plane pulled out of the gate and taxied to the runway, I noticed that my disfigured neighbor was silent, staring out the window, arms folded to cover his mutilated hands. I couldn't help but notice how the features on his face apparently had all been reconstructed. Although he wore sunglasses, they couldn't conceal his eyebrow which was located on his left cheek. The skin on his nose only partially covered his nostrils. His ears were almost nonexistent.

But his hands startled me most. The fingers on both were completely gone. The left one was just a stub from his knuckles down, and the skin was so thin that it appeared transparent. It looked like the doctors simply stretched what little skin he had left to cover his exposed hand. The right one was in the same condition, but even worse. It was bent back against his arm and looked as if he were trying to touch his elbow.

Sitting next to this man, I began to experience a number

of emotions: thankfulness (that I was in one piece), compassion, and curiosity. I wondered what had happened to reshape this young man's body. I wanted to talk with him . . . but what if he rejected me? I'd feel like a jerk for intruding in his life. But I felt that familiar nudge from the Lord to at least try.

So I began a conversation. He said his name was Johnny, and he had just been to Tucson to visit his girlfriend. *She must be quite a woman,* I thought.

When I apologetically asked if he would mind sharing his tragedy, he quickly responded, "No, not at all. I'd much rather have you talk *with* me than stare *at* me." As I picked my pride up off the floor, he energetically began to tell me his story.

In 1975 he and his father were taking a rest stop at a gas station in Eagle Pass, between Mexico and Texas. While they were waiting outside, a car pulled out in front of a gas-tanker truck. Avoiding the collision, the truck, full of fuel, jackknifed, rolled, and burst into flames, covering approximately seventy people with burning fuel. Johnny and his father were immediately covered and ignited. When I asked about Johnny's hands, I was awed by his reply. While engulfed in flames, Johnny saw an old man pinned on the ground by a steel rod across his chest. Johnny walked over to the man and lifted the rod off his chest, literally burning his own fingers off. I now had a genuine love and respect for this courageous man.

He went on to tell me that he had spent more than three years in the hospital. Upon being released, he had spent another four years in seclusion, due to the scars from his burns. A girl he met during that time unconditionally loved him back into society.

He went on to explain that since that time he has had more than 130 operations—most to just keep him alive. Later that summer, Johnny was to receive a pair of artificial hands.

After he finished telling me his story, I asked him if he had ever considered God during his trauma. He said he had, but as we continued talking he said he had never heard of having a personal relationship with God through Jesus Christ. He wanted to know personally the God who had spared his life. As I shared "The Four Spiritual Laws" booklet with him he was very attentive. He was eager to know of God's forgiveness and love. As the plane landed in San Antonio, Johnny prayed with me, placing his faith in Christ as Savior and Lord.

And so for Johnny, there was a moment in 1975 when he

saw his physical body nearly destroyed. All the medical technology in the world could not and will not make him a whole person. But there was another moment in 1987 when Johnny trusted Christ, and instantaneously God renewed his soul and gave him the promise that his body shall be made new at the coming of Christ.

Maybe you're like me. At times I've been nudged by the Holy Spirit to share Christ with others, but I rationalize away my responsibility to say anything. I wonder if the reason we see so little of the supernatural occurring in our lives is because we are unwilling to take the risks that come with walking and living by faith. We fear the rejection of man more than we fear displeasing God.

Bill's story has nudged me to pray more for the salvation of my neighbor, to ask a waitress at Wendy's if she knew the Man who made Christmas famous, and to talk more with my children about how they can be missionaries in their schools. In short, I've become more acutely aware that God sets up divine appointments for me. And I don't want to miss a single one. Not a one.

25.

Choose Your Rut Carefully

Have you thought lately about where you're going in life?

People. Creatures of habit. Too many of us live like the sign on the rugged Alaskan Highway:

> CHOOSE YOUR RUT CAREFULLY . . .
> YOU'LL BE IN IT FOR THE NEXT 200 MILES

Let's admit it. We like ruts . . . especially comfortable ones. It has been said that a rut is nothing more than a grave with both ends knocked out. Predictable and familiar, ruts offer us security. Like a numbing narcotic, however, they cause us to waste a lot of our lives.

Children naturally resist ruts. As Barbara and I attempt to raise six, we're challenged by their probing questions. We're told a child asks at least 250,000 questions growing up. No wonder they learn so rapidly . . . and stay out of ruts.

Adults don't ask enough questions. Daily we climb on the merry-go-round of life and ritualistically get off. Dizzy. Too fuzzy in our thinking to ask any profound questions, we continue searching for happiness and significance in all the wrong places. Our insecurities force us to accelerate the pace of our lives with little regard for direction or destination. As one man put it, "Most live a lifetime looking for the pot at the end of the rainbow, only to find a pot of salty liver soup."

The Lost Art of Thinking

In Ecclesiastes, Solomon challenges us to "ponder" and "consider" the ruts in our life. He challenges us to think about where life is found. To stop, get out of the ruts and ponder where we are going. To *think*.

In chapters 1 and 2, Solomon reflects on his own life and where he has sought satisfaction . . . in knowledge and intelligence (1:12-18) . . . in hobbies (2:5-6) . . . in accumulating possessions (2:7-8) . . . and in position in life (2:9).

He finally realizes that a wasted life is one in which the quest for happiness was spent trying to quench an unrelenting thirst for significance and meaning in life. Solomon's conclusion has shouted a mostly unheeded warning through the centuries: "All is vanity when you leave out God."

Solomon's words are like a shaft of light breaking into his dark prison of despair: "So I turned to consider wisdom" (2:12).

In a word, Solomon stopped pursuing and started *thinking*. He thought seriously about life through God's eyes.

We don't like to think. It's too hard. There aren't enough immediate results in thinking. We don't know how. We don't have time. Quiet, reflective silence is as endangered as the bald eagle. I heard this thought somewhere: We can live for a few minutes without air, for a few days without water, for a couple of months without food, and for a lifetime without an original thought.

The Questions I'm Asking

Like Solomon, I'm starting to re-learn the lost art of *thinking* . . . of thinking *right* about life. Do you want to know some of the questions I'm wrestling with right now?

What do I *really* believe?

Why am I doing what I'm doing?

What drives me?

What really has brought satisfaction to my life?

What creates pressure in my life? And what does God want me to do about it? (Is it right to have that pressure?)

What really *is* valuable in life?

How does my schedule reflect my ultimate values?

How will my present lifestyle affect my family in twenty years?

What does God want me to do with my life, my family, and my possessions?

I'm learning that thinking is sometimes gritty, lonesome work. The Lord has encouraged me that He is still in the business of creating: new original thoughts . . . life-changing ideas . . . innovations that will redirect our families and shape the destiny of our homes. I'm learning that real thinking is a pioneering work.

Tired of your rut? Are you exhausted because you've tried so many ruts only to find that they all dead-end in the same place of emptiness and discontent?

Real significance and contentment come from God. Our culture needs original thinkers who are plugged in to Him, who will "turn to consider wisdom."

I'd like to encourage you to become one of those original thinkers. Turn off the TV, the car radio, shut that book, put down the newspaper and for a few minutes *ponder* the ruts of your life and where those ruts are quickly taking you. Ask yourself some of the questions I've been asking myself lately.

Thinking is hard work, isn't it? But it has its rewards. God wants us to consider what we believe (our convictions) and where we are headed (our purpose).

26.

How to Stay When Others Stray

Why are we surprised, embarrassed, and disheartened when people fail God? And what can we learn from such failures?

*T*he media trial in 1987 of a well-known TV evangelist couple and the exposure of their sins (and later the sins of yet another evangelist) disturbed me deeply.

As I saw the dirty laundry of another believer's life strung out on television and draped over the printed page, I couldn't help but wonder why God let such a man's ministry continue and flourish for so long. I wondered, *Who really lives the Christian life, not just the glossy, air-brushed and choreographed performance on TV?* I wondered how a person could teach God's truth while apparently living a lie. I wondered how unbelievers were processing the knowledge that one more Christian had failed.

And, more importantly, I wondered if there's any area in my life that is not under the authority of Christ.

What should be our response to scandals in the Christian ministry?

Are we to judge Christianity on the performance of its people?

Should we be surprised when people fail?

Should we be embarrassed and silent?

Should we question God and His work?

Should we gossip further on what the press reports?

Should we stop giving financially to various ministries?

Should those of us in the ministry quit?

Should we become skeptics and cynical about everyone in the ministry?

Should we become disillusioned with Christian men and women? With ministry? With God?

Should we grieve for God and with God? His reputation has once again been tarnished by His children.

And should we grieve especially for immature believers who are shaken to the core by such news?

I'm saddened for new Christians who have recently cut their spiritual molars and are now wondering what have they committed themselves to.

Scandals rage. Bad news always does.

Most importantly I wonder what God wants to say to all of us through this mess. What kind of lives should we live? Is there too much hype and not enough substance to the faith of those who speak from the pulpits about the Christian faith?

Surprised by Sin

We shouldn't be surprised at people's sin. Isn't Scripture replete with realistic descriptions of mankind? Didn't the disciples fail miserably? What would the media have done with King David's affair with Bathsheba and his subsequent murder of her husband? David had a pretty good-sized ministry, too. But we are surprised, aren't we?

Jeremiah gives us a realistic appraisal of our flesh: "The heart is more deceitful than all else and is desperately sick; who can understand it?" (Jeremiah 17:9)

Does this mean we shouldn't trust people, especially those in the ministry? No, but it does mean we shouldn't place our *ultimate* hope in people. We're not that different from David. Each of us is one step away from falling into David's footprints.

The prophet Jeremiah proclaimed a statement that will never appear on the front page of the *New York Times:*

> Thus says the Lord, "Cursed is the man who trusts in mankind, and makes flesh his strength, and whose heart turns away from the Lord. For he will be like a bush in the desert and will not see when prosperity comes, but will live in stony wastes in the wilderness, a land of salt without inhabitant. Blessed is the man who trusts in the Lord and whose trust is the Lord. For he will be like a tree planted by the water, that extends its roots by a stream and will not fear when the heat comes; but its leaves will be green, and it will not be anxious in a year of drought nor cease to yield fruit" (Jeremiah 17:5-8).

The person who places his hope in man will be disappointed every time.

A Godly Perspective

Dozens of thoughts have ricocheted around in my head. I want to share six of them with you. It seems we all need a fresh dose of God's perspective on the immorality that has taken place. We've heard enough of the other side!

1. *I am reminded that I need to be accountable to Christ and a few others for my life.* I need to submit my life to people who will keep me honest and tell me what I need to hear. "Iron sharpening iron."

I see some who apparently think that isolation from others represents safety. And that being aloof and insulated from others keeps them from being hurt. But I've been reminded that there is no real security to the person who is afraid to be known and is always distancing himself from others. I've seen that protection is never guaranteed by walking into enemy territory alone. And perspective about life is elusive to the person who must ask and answer all his own questions about himself.

In my life, accountability to others works like gravity — it holds me to the truth. Paul knew its importance. Look at this command: "And be subject to one another in the fear of Christ" (Ephesians 5:20). Who are your protectors? Do they include your mate and a close friend?

2. *We should not lose heart in doing good.* "Therefore, since we have this ministry, as we received mercy, we do not lose heart" (2 Corinthians 4:1).

"And let us not lose heart in doing good, for in due time we shall reap if we do not grow weary. So then, while we have opportunity, let us do good to all men" (Galatians 6:9). We need to be careful not to let others' failures dictate the level of our faith and commitment. It is disheartening to see another fail, but we must keep on running, running to win.

3. *I've realized that I have no right to judge a brother's fall.* Paul said, "I am who I am by the grace of God" (1 Corinthians 15:10). There's no room for pride when you grasp the fact that God's grace puts *all of us* on the same level, depraved yet forgiven sinners.

4. *View the fall of others as an example for us, so that we might not fall into temptation.* "Now these things happened as examples

for us, that we should not crave evil things, as they also craved" (1 Corinthians 10:6). This was written of the Israelites who, after being led out of slavery by God, became idolaters and immoral. And because of their lack of belief, they never entered the land God had promised to give them. God disqualified them. Playing patty-cake with sin results in death.

5. *God will reward those who faithfully follow Jesus Christ and who live their life to be pleasing to Him.* "Therefore also we have as our ambition, whether at home or absent, to be pleasing to Him. For we must all appear before the judgment seat of Christ, that each one may be recompensed for his deeds in the body, according to what he has done, whether good or bad" (2 Corinthians 5:9-10). Everything about you and me will be revealed on that day. Everything. God *will* purge and *reward*.

6. *Live your life as though Christ were coming back today.* "But the day of the Lord will come like a thief, in which the heavens will pass away with a roar and the elements will be destroyed with intense heat, and the earth and its works will be burned up. Since all these things are to be destroyed in this way, what sort of people ought you to be in holy conduct and godliness?" (2 Peter 3:10-11). Will you answer that question today?

The preacher in Ecclesiastes adds this: "The conclusion, when all has been heard is: Fear God and keep His commandments, because this applies to every person. Because God will bring every act to judgment, everything which is hidden, whether it is good or evil" (Ecclesiastes 12:13-14).

But perhaps the best word about how to stay when others stray is from Jesus Christ. John 21:18-23 records a dialogue between Peter and our Lord. Peter was raising a question about another one of the disciples. He was in essence asking Christ what this other disciple ought to do. "Lord," Peter said (comparing his life with the other man), "what about this man?"

Jesus said to him, "If I want him to remain until I come, what is that to you? *You follow Me!*"

Enough said.

27.

R.I.P.

*What do you think your last words would be
if you knew they would be your last?*

Is there something innately a part of our human nature that causes us to want to collect things? I read in a magazine article that there are all kinds of interesting collections today: oil paintings, sculptures, political campaign buttons, guns, stamps, coins.

Francis Johnson of Darwin, Minnesota, has collected string since 1950. His ball of string measures over ten feet in diameter and weighs five tons.

One collector recently paid three million dollars for a collection of baseball cards, then sold them for four million dollars.

Canadian sailor Joe Simmons, who died in 1965, boasted nearly 5,000 tattoos.

There's a man in New Orleans with 129 Corvairs, and a Dallas man I met ten years ago who has collected more than 4,000 hotel keys (he told me of another collector who had made off with more than 10,000). I've even heard of a collection of the addresses of famous people — 3,500 listings.

But perhaps the prize for the most unusual collection of all time goes to Italian dentist Giovanni Battista Orsenigo who by 1903 had a collection of 2,000,744 teeth. How would you like to have been one of his patients?

Yes, I admit: I still bring home to my kids matchbooks, menus and bars of soap from hotels I visit. And I have to confess that I have a small and strange collection of my own: "exit lines" or the final utterances of dying men.

The Last Bookend

My collection of quotes is not as morbid as you may think. I've observed that these terminal lines are in many cases a summary statement of the life of the person speaking them. They not only tell you how a man died, but also how he lived. These last words are the bookend of the legacy a person leaves.

Consider the last words and legacy of these men.

Henry David Thoreau, the writer who was know as a stubborn, arrogant individualist (he is said to have loved a snowstorm more than Christ, and wanted nothing to do with the church), died on May 6, 1862. Shortly before his death, his aunt asked him if he'd made his peace with God. Thoreau responded, "I didn't know we'd ever quarreled."

Contrast Thoreau's cynicism with the inspiring last words of the great evangelist, D. L. Moody. He was reported to have turned to his sons by his bedside and said, "If God be your partner, make your plans large."

I've observed two contrasting themes in the words spoken by those who are near death's door. One is hopelessness, ominous and depressing whispers of a feared fate. The other is hopefulness, which gleefully shouts its confident message: "This isn't it! Death is not the end — it's the beginning!"

Ponder this contrast in the deathbed quotes below:

"Bring down the curtain — the farce is over" — Sixteenth-century French philosopher and comic, Francois Rabelais.

"Our God is the God from whom cometh salvation. God is the Lord by whom we escape death" — Martin Luther.

* * *

"I am abandoned by God and man! I shall go to hell! O Christ, O Jesus Christ!" — Voltaire.

"I enjoy heaven already in my soul. My prayers are all converted into praises" — Augustus Toplady, author of the great hymn "Rock of Ages."

* * *

"I would give worlds, if I had them, if *The Age of Reason* had never been published. O Lord, help me! Christ, help me! Stay with me! It is hell to be left alone!" — Thomas Paine, whose work *The Age of Reason* attempted to refute the Bible.

"I have pain — but I have peace, I have peace" — Richard Baxter, seventeeth-century Puritan theologian.

* * *

"I am convinced that there is no hope" — Winston Churchill, whose vision and battle cry in life was to "never give up."

"Live in Christ, die in Christ, and the flesh need not fear death" — John Knox, Scottish church reformer.

* * *

"When I lived, I provided for everything but death; now I must die, and I am unprepared to die" — Cesare Borgia, Fifteenth-century Italian archbishop.

Billy Graham notes that when the great saint Joseph Everett was dying, he continued exclaiming, "GLORY! GLORY! GLORY!" for more than twenty-five minutes until he breathed his last.

*   *   *

Edgar Allen Poe, who is said to have lived an erratic life of lies and drunkenness, died in 1849 at age forty after being found lying in a street. His last words: "Lord, help my poor soul!"

August Strindberg, a Swedish dramatist, died with a Bible clasped tightly to his chest, saying, "It is atoned for."

*   *   *

In the Bible, the last recorded words spoken by Judas Iscariot were, "I have sinned in that I have betrayed innocent blood." He then went out and hanged himself.

As he was being stoned to death, Stephen, the church's first martyr, fell to his knees and cried out, "Lord, do not hold this sin against them!"

Visiting Death's Door

You may wonder: Why the visit to death's door?

Ecclesiastes 7:2 tells us, "It is better to go to a house of mourning, than to go to a house of feasting, because that is the end of every man, *and the living takes it to heart.*"

What do you think your last words would be if you knew they would be your last? How would they be a summary of your life?

The legacy you are passing on to your children and others is the life you are living today. Read the first fourteen verses of Ecclesiastes 7, and especially note verse 12: "Wisdom preserves the life of its possessors." You and I need wisdom, skill in everyday living, if we are to live a life that is pleasing to God and leave a legacy of right choices.

Perhaps we should consider the last words of Jesus Christ, who, even in His death, taught us how to live and what our priorities ought to be:

"IT IS FINISHED."

Here are the three most profound words in all of human history. Sin had been paid for "in full" with a life and love that demands our obedience.

Have you experienced the forgiveness of the Son of God and the "finished" work of Jesus Christ on the cross? How then will you live?

After His resurrection, while standing on the Mount of Olives before departing for heaven in a cloud, Christ gave us a profound promise and command by which to measure our lives: "But you shall receive power when the Holy Spirit has come upon you; and you shall be my witnesses . . . even to the remotest part of the earth" (Acts 1:8).

What is your response to His life? His death? His command to tell others the gospel?

What will be your final words? How do you want to be remembered?

How is your life today another investment in the legacy you leave?

Will you measure your life by the world's yardstick or by Christ's words?

If Christ is not *Lord of your life today,* then what guarantee is there that you will be a person of "hopefulness" when you die?

P·A·R·T · T·H·R·E·E

Pulling Weeds, Planting Seeds

In My Walk With God

28.

From Mission Field to Missionary

*How I was lured from my trivial pursuits
to a pursuit of holiness.*

As a college student, I lived my life in two different spiritual conditions. For the first two years I was a mission field; the last two years I was a missionary. Without a doubt I can say I enjoyed the second condition more: being on assignment from God, sent for a specific task and purpose.

Ever since my junior year in college more than twenty years ago, I've sought daily to give my life to Jesus Christ, to be His tool, to be used as He thinks best. That, my friend, is both thrilling and peaceful. Let me explain.

I'd given my life to many lesser pursuits in high school and college. I was a Christian, but it was just fire insurance. I believed Christ died only to save me from eternal condemnation, nothing more.

As great a man as Jesus was, I had learned to treat Him simply as a spare tire. When a crisis arose, I'd bring Him out and ask for His help. When the crisis passed, He was once again relegated to the trunk.

Then in college, I achieved almost every goal I'd set: honors and acceptance in the "in-crowd," tangible achievements for all to see. It really didn't matter that I was on top of only a small heap. I was on top!

Yet spiritually I felt on the bottom. My life was empty. Living had no purpose. I realized that even if I achieved the ultimate dream of some — being President of the United States — my life would still be empty. I had come to a simple conclusion: Fulfillment isn't found in achieving, succeeding, or accumulating.

So, at the age of twenty I began to grapple with the truth about life.

Then I met a Person who transformed my life from grey, dull, drab purposelessness into the technicolor, stereophonic thrill of knowing God and of following His plan for my life.

Please note: I met a *Person*. I didn't learn a set of two-thousand-year-old precepts or a rigid collection of dogma to hang my hat on. Nor was it a sterile doctrine that challenged my heart. It wasn't law. It was love . . . the personified love of God manifested in the Person of Jesus Christ.

It was a Person . . . the God-Man. The Person who had absolute authority over my life. The Person who loved me and died for me. The Person who had loved me even during all those years when I relegated Him to spare-tire status.

That love, demonstrated by the "Hound of Heaven," began to chase me. It lured me from all the lesser loyalties and my trivial pursuits.

Slowly, ever so slowly, that love softened a calloused, proud heart and caused it to repent. His love motivated me to confess my sins of selfishness and my petty plans in favor of a life designed by God.

Giving Up

I exchanged my spiritual poverty for a destiny determined by the King of kings. But I had to submit. I had to give up, give in, and give all to Christ.

The same Lord who died upon the cross was alive and pleading with me through His understanding eyes, "I died for you. Will you live for me?"

Through the Scriptures the love of Christ came alive. No longer did Christianity mean stale, boring rituals; instead, it was a refreshing relationship with Christ, and a knowledge of His appointed purpose for my life.

John Wesley wrote: "Give me one hundred men who fear nothing but God, who hate nothing but sin, and who know nothing but Jesus Christ and Him crucified, and I will shake the world."

Questions to contemplate:

1. Am I experiencing, avoiding, or ignoring the love of God manifested through Christ Jesus?

2. Is He Lord over every area of my life?

3. Am I in the center of God's will for my life? Is my career a trivial pursuit, or is it God's approved choice for me?

4. What do I need to do with the rest of my life? How does my life presently reflect my priorities and life plan?

My friend, the world needs to be shaken. Christ the man, Christ the Savior, is Christ the revolutionary. Are you part of His revolution or are you in need of being revolutionized? Are you willing to be one of His hundred? Are you a mission field or a missionary?

29.

Life Isn't Fair—
But the Master Is

What to do when the green film of envy blurs your vision.

I may never buy another Hershey's chocolate candy bar for my kids to split. I'm not referring to the solid milk chocolate one with squares, but the one with almonds. There is absolutely no way to break it into *equal shares*.

My children's cries of injustice erupt as soon as they receive their portion: "NOT FAIR! Benjamin got a bigger piece," cries one child, as the exasperating whine of another announces, "Ashley got three almonds. I didn't get any. It's NOT FAIR!"

Our standard and dispassionate response to them has become, "That's right, LIFE ISN'T FAIR!"

But we also devised a solution: We let one of them break the candy bar in half, and then the other child gets to pick the portion *he* thinks is bigger. It's fascinating to watch them cut the candy bar with the attention and precision of a surgeon to ensure that the other doesn't get too much.

I wish fairness in all of life could be solved that easily. Most things, however, do not divide in equal portions.

Life just isn't fair.

Sometimes our "portion" in life seems downright bitter. It just doesn't seem fair that:

- a divorced mother of three preschoolers should have to work two part-time jobs and raise her children alone while her irresponsible ex-husband parties and plays and neglects the child support.
- a thirty-four-year-old missionary and father of two little girls, ages two and four, should die suddenly of a heart attack while on vacation with his family.
- a ten-year-old boy is killed by a drunk driver while the driver "suffers" only bruised ribs and a hang-over.
- a child has an operation on his appendix and gets AIDS through a disease-infected blood transfusion.

Left to my human reason, these painfully unjust circumstances don't seem to resemble even remotely our standard of "fairness." They make me angry. They cause me to question, to wonder, and to shake my head.

The Fairness of It All

Fortunately, most of us face unfairness on less tragic levels. But our own experience is very real, and we, too, are left to wonder about "the fairness of it all." Do you ever struggle over:

- Why you're not more gifted or more decisive?

- Why you're considered too old or too young for a key position that opened up at work?

- Why a less productive employee at work gets a raise and you don't?

- Why you aren't a better conversationalist, or don't feel free to laugh?

- Why others who can have children don't, and you aren't able to have children?

- Why you tend to get angry at those you love the most?

- Why you had a difficult relationship with one or both of your parents, while others you know grew up in happy homes?

- Why you aren't more physically attractive?

- Why "cheaters" prosper and get more, while you're honest but seem to have less?

Life isn't fair.

Life doesn't always deliver equal identical portions for everyone. We arrogantly presume that we are the best judges of fairness and equality. Our problem is that we live in the dimension of time and see only today, while the One who weaves the tapestry of our lives does so with eternal purposes in mind. Our limited perspective leads us to compare what we *think* we deserve with what others *appear* to get. The inevitable result is *envy.*

Jesus offers a parable dealing with fairness in Matthew 20:1-16 that could be entitled "Life Isn't Fair, But the Master *Is!*" It's a parable for those who tend to keep a scorecard on life, for those who are tempted to envy others.

Right Motivation

The parable is about a landowner who hired laborers for his vineyard. Early in the morning he hired a few men and agreed to pay them a standard day's wage, which back then was equivalent to about eighteen cents. Throughout the morning and even late into the afternoon, the landowner hired additional laborers. He promised to pay them "whatever is right." They agreed to his terms and went to work.

Later that evening he paid each laborer his wages. He began by paying those who had come last. Although they had worked only a short time, he paid each employee eighteen cents for his labor. Then he paid the other laborers, and each of them also received eighteen cents, though they had all worked a different number of hours.

The men who had been hired first and who had worked diligently all day in the scorching heat complained. "That's not fair!" they grumbled. But the landowner reminded them he had done no wrong. He had paid them what he promised.

The landowner added, "Is it not lawful for me to do what I wish with my own?" Then he put his finger on the real issue: "Or is your *eye envious* because I am generous?" To this they made no response.

Likewise, the laborers who had received a full day's wage for less than a full day's labor were strangely silent. The master gave them more than they deserved. He had shown them grace, unmerited favor.

How to Face Life's Unfairness

I have found at least three principles here that will help us as we face situations that *seem* unfair.

1. *Remember what you really deserve.* The men hired first *expected* a bonus (verse 10). They thought the landowner owed them a "little extra" even though he had promised them no such thing. We also think we deserve more than we actually do.

I have to admit this is occasionally a struggle for me. I look at what I've done for my Master (God), and believe that I deserve more. That's a dangerously wrong evaluation of worth. After all, He gave me everything I have. Plus, Scripture reminds us that what we ultimately deserve is not heaven, but hell.

2. *Envy begins when we compare ourselves with others.* We get into trouble when we look at what others have. We compare and become envious. The laborers' problem was that they saw too much! Their eyes betrayed them.

How's your vision? Can you look clearly at what others have and be glad they have it? Or does the green film of envy blur your vision? How do you handle the news of a friend remodeling her house? Or the promotion of an associate at work? Or the news of your neighbor's child who won an award that your child wanted? Check your vision regularly. Envy can cause spiritual cataracts and blur your vision.

3. *Ultimately we must trust the Master, who owns everything, and be convinced that He knows what He is doing.* God is the Sovereign Ruler of the universe. He alone controls and rules over all. Not only does He know what He is doing, but He also loves us.

Barbara and I want our children to grow up realizing God won't give each of them the same share of earthly benefits. But we want them also to know He will always deal with them in perfect judgment and according to His righteous character.

Everything that occurs in their lives will either come directly from God's hands or be gently sifted through His fingers. Everything is for the purpose of shaping their lives in His image. Circumstances, events, and problems may not always appear to be fair, but they have permission to occur from our loving Father.

Life isn't fair. But I know One who is fair. And He can be trusted. Will you trust Him?

"For the Lord your God is the God of gods and the Lord of lords, the great, the mighty, and the awesome God who does not show partiality . . . " (Deuteronomy 10:17).

30.

The University of Adversity

When you graduate, you may find yourself closer to God than when you were schooled in pleasure and abundance.

This life we live is made up of all kinds of apparent contradictions. Solomon preached about one of these in the book of Ecclesiastes:

Prosperity is not necessarily good,
and adversity is not necessarily bad.

Solomon was qualified to preach on the subject. He experienced to the hilt both prosperity and adversity. He was unbelievably wealthy, yet he died in despair. In 1 Kings 4:21-28 it is recorded that Solomon was truly the first "fat cat." He had power, prestige, luxury, and uncounted wealth. His posh palace was the daily scene of incredible feasts where he fed hundreds of people.

Wouldn't you enjoy living like Solomon? Of course you would. Who wouldn't? But in the fifth, sixth, and seventh chapters of Ecclesiastes Solomon shouts his warning:

Prosperity and adversity are not necessarily
what they appear to be.

Prosperity Is Not Necessarily Good

Solomon, in Ecclesiastes 5:10-20, shows us that big bucks and possessions actually may keep us from godly introspection. They may numb us, hindering us in knowing the truth of Scripture and applying it to our lives. Affluence may allow us to flatter our bodies with luxury while living lives filled with spiritual mediocrity. It may keep us from questioning the reason for our existence.

The second point of Solomon's sermon on prosperity is found in Ecclesiastes 6:1-6, where he gives us a firm exhortation: Possessions without a clear purpose in life result in emptiness.

A biography of a successful young movie producer, who has created several of the biggest box-office blockbusters of all time, describes him as "restless, unfulfilled, and a frustrated person." His relationship with his wife failed. He can't quit what he is doing, and he *can't enjoy life.* This rich, successful mogul is imprisoned in a cage that he has built. Fame hasn't satisfied. Without God, his cage is truly empty.

Third, Solomon says that riches don't satisfy man's *true* appetite (Ecclesiastes 6:7-9). Ask a rich man if he is content. When multimillionaire John D. Rockefeller was asked how much money it took to satisfy him, he replied: "Just one more dollar than I have."

Wealth is not the ultimate source of gratification.

Solomon continues his message on prosperity in Ecclesiastes

6:10-12 by stating that all abundance and prosperity is meaningless and futile without God. He notes that the man who has prospered has received his reward in full, only to find someday that it is an empty tin cup.

Adversity Is Not Necessarily Bad

Solomon does not leave us reeling from his potent warnings about prosperity. He pulls no punches when he tells us in 7:1-14 that adversity may be our friend.

Look at verses 13 and 14: "Consider the work of God; for who is able to straighten what He has bent? In the day of prosperity be happy, but in the day of adversity consider — God has made one as well as the other, so that man may not discover what will be after him."

In other words, "Enjoy the prosperity while you have it, but don't worship it. Embrace adversity, for as you go into the house of mourning and suffering, you will find yourself closer to God than you were in the house of pleasure and abundance."

In Ecclesiastes 7:2-4 are these words: "It is better to go to the house of mourning than to go to the house of feasting; for this is the end of all men, and the living will take it to heart. Sorrow is better than laughter, for by sadness of countenance the heart is made glad. The heart of the wise is in the house of mourning; but the heart of fools is in the house of pleasure."

Solomon makes his argument crystal clear. Adversity brings perspective. Death may teach us more about life than life itself. Pain is good, for it warns us that not all is right.

Have you ever experienced suffering that brought you to your knees and drastically reduced your options in life? Those were the times when you didn't consider how you were going to spend your extra dollars or extra moments. *Life was reduced to a basic decision: Can God be trusted?*

Solomon explains that adversity calls attention to our priorities. Prosperity confuses us by increasing our choices. Adversity clarifies our alternatives by reducing us to an inescapable dependence on the Lord. Aleksandr Solzhenitsyn, the Russian dissident who spent many years in concentration camps, wrote, "Bless you, prison, for having been in my life." For it was there that Solzhenitsyn found Christ and came into a meaningful relationship with God Himself. He found life while in the crucible of adversity, not a place where you and I would want to look for meaning and fulfillment.

The Lesson Plans

Emerging from Solomon's life are several lessons we need to consider. We should wear the cloak of materialism loosely. We must consider its choking influence on our hunger and thirst for godliness and pursuit of Christ.

We need to give our children a legacy of life, truth, and warm family memories, not just an inheritance of wealth and possessions. What kind of values are we passing on to our children? They will imitate what you and I model. Do we want our kids to be comfortable and compassionless . . . or do we want them to be godly and Christ-centered, people of value rather than people of success?

When God allows adversity in our life, we must embrace it. Learn from it. We would be foolish to waste any of what God wants to teach us as He gets our attention and brings us close to His heart.

C. S. Lewis summed up these three chapters of Ecclesiastes when he wrote, "God whispers to us in our pleasure, he speaks to us in our joys, but he shouts to us in our sorrow. Problems are God's megaphones to a deaf world to get our attention."

Prosperity can cause us to lose focus and forget our priorities. It is through adversity that we learn what is of true worth and value.

31.

The Mighty Rescue Attempt

Planting the seeds for spiritual harvest.

The year was 1940. The French army had just collapsed under the siege of Hitler's onslaught. The Dutch had folded, overwhelmed by the Nazi regime. The Belgians had surrendered. And the British army was trapped on the coast of France in the channel port of Dunkirk.

Two hundred twenty thousand of Britain's finest young men seemed doomed to die, to turn the English Channel red with their blood. The Fuehrer's troops, only miles away in the hills of France, didn't realize how close to victory they actually were.

Any rescue seemed feeble and futile in the time remaining. A "thin" British navy — "the professional warlords" — told King George VI that at best they could save 17,000 troops. The House of Commons was warned to prepare for "hard and heavy tidings."

Politicians stood paralyzed. The King reigned powerless. And the Allies were relegated to watching, as spectators from a distance. Then, as the doom of the British army seemed imminent, a strange fleet appeared on the horizon of the English Channel, perhaps the wildest assortment of boats ever assembled in history. Trawlers, tugs, scows, fishing sloops, lifeboats, pleasure craft, smacks, coasters, sailboats, an island ferry by the name of *Gracie Fields,* even the America's Cup challenger *Endeavor,* plus the London fire brigade flotilla. Each ship was manned by civilian volunteers, English fathers sailing to rescue Britain's exhausted, bleeding sons.

In his epic book *The Last Lion: Visions of Glory 1874-1932,* William Manchester writes that what happened in 1940 in less than twenty-four hours still seems like a miracle. Not only were all of the British soldiers rescued, but numerous Allied troops as well. More than 338,000 troops were redeemed that day.

A Modern-day Challenge

Allow me to suggest a parallel for today. For too long the paid professionals (ministers, missionaries, and full-time Christian workers) have unknowingly robbed laymen of the great privilege of leading others to Christ. But today, like the leaders of Britain during that crisis, pastors and Christian leaders need civilian volunteers to sign up for a rescue effort of even greater magnitude.

For too long Christians have compromised their message of salvation. When an opportunity arises for confronting a spiritual subject we squirm uncomfortably and mumble something about church (not Christ). We often go to great lengths to avoid asking another person about his eternal destiny and his relationship with Jesus Christ.

I'm amazed at how concerned I am with what a friend, neighbor or associate may think of me. Why are we so preoccupied with another's possible rejection of us when, humanly speaking, his soul may be hanging in the balance? Perhaps our focus is on the wrong thing.

Bedrock Obedience

On a recent flight to the West Coast, I talked to a "yuppie of yuppies." He had life wired to 220 volts! He was all together, and he looked the part. Though I was tempted to say nothing "spiritual" after spending an hour getting to know the young man, I finally asked him about his religious beliefs. The fact that he sinned didn't matter to him. The fact God would hold him accountable didn't concern him. And the fact that hell exists didn't bother him either. But it certainly bothered me. Before we landed, I had the opportunity to sensitively and clearly present the person of Jesus Christ and His plan for salvation to him.

He said he wasn't interested. But I had been faithful, my mission in that man's life for that particular day was accomplished. In the words of Bill Bright, founder and president of Campus Crusade for Christ, "Successful witnessing is simply taking the initiative to share Christ in the power of the Holy Spirit, and leaving the results to God." Yes, I struggle with turning a conversation to spiritual things. However, I've found a few facts that compel me to ask others about their spiritual condition.

First, I am compelled by the realization that without Christ all men are lost and without hope. Man continues to fail. Sure, humans do good things, but that doesn't change the fact that we all sin naturally. I've never taught a single one of our six children how to steal a cookie, yet they all have done it. It is part of their nature. As a result, they are sinners. And sinners need forgiveness to have hope.

Second, I'm compelled to share Christ with others because of the reality of hell. Thinking about hell is not in vogue today. You'll never see an Academy Award-winning movie on hell, or hear a popular song describing what is reserved for those who are outside a personal faith in Jesus Christ. And it isn't spoken of much from our pulpits, either. But the place of eternal judgment and torment is more real than the room you are in right now. I may not like the fact that it exists, and I may even try to ignore it. But that doesn't change the truth that hell *does* exist, and people who die without Christ will spend eternity there.

Third, I want to share the Good News because it is the very reason for which Christ came to the planet Earth. Christ came "to seek and to save the lost." Since He is the Master and I am His slave, shouldn't I be about the Master's business daily? And since the Master, Jesus Christ, lives inside of me, shouldn't I allow Him, even help Him, continue His work of seeking and saving the lost through my life?

Jesus Christ didn't go to the cross just so we could enjoy happy homes and fellowship in a holy huddle. He didn't die and bear the sins of the world just so your sex life would be satisfying. And He didn't suffer the severance of His relationship with the Father and enter into death's clutches so that we could eat, drink and be merry and fulfill the American dream.

He came to *seek* and to *save* those who were lost.

Look around you. Are the people in your neighborhood morally stronger than they were ten years ago? What have you done to make a difference? The Army of God needs fresh troops who are willing to get into a foxhole. The enemy is real. The message is more powerful. The hour couldn't be more urgent. And your family is an important part of the solution.

Love Is Active

"So what do I do?" you ask. Below are a few ideas. Don't let this list overwhelm you. The important thing is to start . . . somewhere . . . with something. An individual can't do everything, but you *can* do something; and together, we will make a difference.

1. Read Bill Bright's award-winning book *Witnessing Without Fear*. It will show you how to share your faith with con-

fidence in any type of witnessing situation.

2. Have an evangelistic dinner party at your home for a few couples you know.

3. Host a Good News Club for children in your neighborhood. I'm praying God will use us in the Family Ministry in the next twenty-five years to see a revival of child evangelism. Contrary to our culture's belief, children *are* valuable.

4. Pick up several copies of "The Four Spiritual Laws" at your local Christian bookstore. Leave some on your desk for people to pick up and read. Put some in your pocket or purse and share them or give them away as you go about your errands. Then ask those same people later what they thought of the booklet. America needs to be confronted with Jesus Christ on a personal level.

5. Show your children how to share their faith. Invite a neighborhood child to go to church with you.

6. Together with a friend, host an "evangelistic coffee" (perhaps with a holiday theme) for your neighbors and friends.

7. Show the HomeBuilders Film Series in your church and lead a HomeBuilders Couple Series with your neighbors.

8. And finally, promise yourself that you will *try* to share Christ with the next person you sit beside on a plane, bus, or train.

Why not make your growing Christian home the springboard for sharing the greatest news the world has ever heard?

"The people who know their God will display strength and take action" (Daniel 11:32b).

32.

Gripes, Grumbles, and Grouches

Griping and complaining are weeds that must be pulled quickly.

Do you ever get annoyed with the complaining around your house? I do. We gripe about who gets to sit where at the dinner table. We grumble about chores, especially who cleans up after dinner. We get grumpy over socks that never match, toilets that aren't flushed, toys that populate the floor, and tubs that are littered with assorted dolls, boats, bottles, and melting bars of soap.

It became so bad about a year ago that we memorized Philippians 2:14: "Do all things without grumbling or disputing." That helped. For a while.

But recently grumbling became so prevalent again that I felt as if someone had delivered a batch of bad attitudes to our house. Like sulfuric acid, complaining can eat away at whatever it splashes on. Complaining corrodes joy and dissolves good attitudes. Spiritually, it's dangerous and deadly.

The Bible speaks of complaining in picturesque language. The Hebrew word for complain, *anan*, means "to sigh habitually." When we complain or "sigh," its like letting the air out of a tire; we can stop all forward progress if enough air escapes.

In the New Testament the Greek word *memps* means "finding fault with one's lot." Do you ever feel your circumstances just aren't fair? Do you ever find fault with what God is doing in your life? What He's bringing your way?

If you have a problem with grumbling, you're not alone. The Old Testament book of Numbers could easily be renamed *The Grumbler Chronicles*. The children of Israel grumbled against Moses, Aaron and God. They didn't like manna, so they complained: "Manna for breakfast, manna for lunch, manna for dinner! Is this all we get, this manna?"

So God gave them quail. They had quail boiled and broiled, quail under glass, quail a la cactus, quail nuggets, and probably even McQuail burgers until they were sick of it. Can you empathize with them? We who live in America are used to an almost limitless variety of culinary delights. So what if they griped a little? A little complaining is understandable, isn't it?

Complaining: No Trivial Matter

But the complaining by the children of Israel wasn't a trivial matter, and God didn't view it lightly. Why? *They complained about the provision and the will of God.* His daily supernatural provision and guidance was criticized and rejected by ungrateful people.

I wonder what we would find if we performed open-heart surgery on a complainer. Exploratory surgery would reveal that grumbling can be a form of heart disease, "rebellion against authority" (see Job 23:2). At other times, complaining is a loss of perspective, a failure to remember who is in control. It's an attitude that questions, "Does God really know what's best for me?"

Jude 16 tells us that complaining germinates in a selfish heart: "These are grumblers, finding fault, following after their own lusts . . . " But generally a complainer is a person who is dissatisfied with his lot in life, the circumstances God has allowed to come his way. The children of Israel's grumbling was only symptomatic of a far more fatal disease: unbelief, a lack of faith that God knew what He was doing.

A Heart Attitude

Griping and complaining are vocal amplifiers of one's heart-attitude.

What was God's prescription for this heart problem? Let's look at how He responded in Numbers 11:1.

> Now the people became like those who complain of adversity in the hearing of the Lord; and when the Lord heard it, His anger was kindled, and the fire of the Lord burned among them and consumed some of the outskirts of the camp.

God judged the sin in their midst. Later, the earth gobbled up a few hundred of them, fire turned another group into cinders, and poisonous serpents killed thousands . . . all because of their complaining.

What's the solution for us gripers?

First, we need to realize that complaining is dangerous. We have seen a number of Christian leaders fall into immorality. I wonder how many more Christians have been declared "unusable" by God because of their complaining? We know the enemy of our souls doesn't want us to fulfill God's intended purpose for our lives. If he can't derail us through lust or immorality in our private lives, then the cunning devil of hell will seek a different bait for his trap. For many of us, that snare is the temptation to gripe, grumble, and complain against God (1 Corinthians 9:24 — 10:13). Illicit sex is not the only sin that derails Christians.

Second, we need to remember that God knows what He is doing. Joseph puts me under the pile. He was tossed into a pit by his brothers, sold by them into slavery, unjustly accused of fooling around with Potiphar's wife, thrown into prison, and forgotten by a friend he had helped. Yet Scripture doesn't record a single complaint from his lips.

He could have become bitter against his brothers, but he didn't. He could have smashed his fist against the prison walls and complained that his circumstances were unjust, but he didn't.

What was the secret of his complaint-free life? The answer is in Genesis 45:5-8 where we find Joseph, now the governor of Egypt, addressing his starving brothers. "And now do not be grieved or angry with yourselves," he begins, "because God has sent me before you to preserve life." Three times in four verses Joseph says, "God sent me here." His was a perspective that comes as a result of an uncommon faith in an omnipotent God. Joseph grasped the truth that God is in control, and that He knows what He is doing.

Third, we need to put away past complaints that may have become bitterness. A grudge is an aging complaint still being held against another person. The longer you carry a complaint against another, the greater the probability it will become a grudge too heavy to handle. Complaining can give birth to resentment. "Be hospitable to one another without complaint" (1 Peter 4:9).

If you have a complaint against a brother, go to him in private and clear the slate.

Fourth, we need to keep "giving thanks in all things" (1 Thessalonians 5:16). Jesus gave the disciples a "test" of their faith by putting them in a little boat, in a big sea, in a raging storm. The disciples complained that they were perishing, instead of acknowledging God's sovereignty and trusting Him.

I'm sorry to say that I seem to flunk more of these "faith tests" than I pass. God wants me to see Him in the midst of my circumstances, to trust Him, without having the outcome clearly presented in front of me. God says, "You must believe in Me before you see it," but I say, "Let me see all that's going on here, and then I'll believe it!" My unbelief shows when I fail to give thanks in all things.

We will never be able to genuinely give thanks unless we acknowledge God as the sovereign ruler of the universe, at work in our lives through our circumstances.

Are you satisfied with what God has provided for you today (your mate, your children, your circumstances, your home, your job, your boss, your income)?

Does God know what He is doing in your life?

Can you give thanks, right now, for God's will and provision for your life?

The challenge is to pull those grumbling, complaining weeds out of our thoughts and attitudes and mouths, and replace them by planting soothing seeds of thankfulness.

33.

The Marathon

Take heed, lest you, too, should be disqualified.

Joggers make me feel guilty. I had lunch once with a serious runner, a world-class ultra-marathoner (they run more than one marathon at a time). Max Hooper has a unique will to win.

After surgery on both knees, Max was told he would never run again. Three months later he ran a 2:47 marathon and qualified for the Boston Marathon. Since then he's run in four additional Boston Marathons. He has competed in six Pikes Peak Marathons. I get light-headed just thinking of *driving* up there!

He was one of 410 men who qualified for the world championship for ultra-marathoners, the Western States 100-Mile Run from Squaw Valley, California, to Auburn, California. Only 210 finished the race because of extreme temperature changes, rugged terrain and altitude sickness. He prevented dehydration by consuming more than 50 pounds of liquid during the race.

But Max's ultimate race was completed on his fortieth birthday in some of the most hostile environments our planet could offer a runner. The start: Badwater, California, in the oven of Death Valley, 282 feet below sea level, the lowest point in the United States. The finish: the refrigerated summit of Mount Whitney at 14,494 feet, the highest altitude in the contiguous United States. Total distance: 146 miles.

Max and a Marine buddy started the race by moonlight in the one-hundred-degree desert floor of Death Valley. They began by hurdling sidewinders and ended by scrambling on all fours up a glacier. They ran the last six hours of the race above 10,000 feet. Yes, they did sleep. They took two eight-hour rest breaks. They completed the task in sixty-three hours, twelve minutes—an American record. Max wore out three pairs of running shoes and his feet swelled two sizes by the time he reached the summit.

Max said that he was able to finish this incredible race because he didn't run alone.

The Race Is On

You and I run in a similar race. It's a race that God has set before each of us, and it takes place on a course of extremes. There's the agony of the valleys contrasted with the summits of joy. We face miles of rugged terrain and climate changes in between. Life is a race for every Christian. It is a race you and I must finish . . . and win.

How are you running today? Are you winning or losing? Did you know the omnipotent God of the universe has instructed us on how to win this race?

> Do you not know that those who run in a race *all run*, but only one receives the price? *Run in such a way that you may*

win. And everyone who competes in the games exercises self-control in all things. They then do it to receive a perishable wreath, but we are imperishable. Therefore, I run in such a way, as not without aim; I box in such a way, as not beating the air; but I buffet my body and make it my slave, *lest possibly, after I have preached to others I myself should be disqualified* (1 Corinthians 9:24-27).

Notice the first verse, "Those who run in a race all run." Did you realize that you're included in this race? What kind of runner are you? In the Christian life, there are at least five kinds of runners:

The Casual Runner. He runs when he feels like it and when conditions are perfect. For these Christians, the sacrifice demanded by the race is just too high.

The Cautious Runner. He thinks a lot about the race. But he plays it safe and seldom leaves the starting blocks.

The Compromised Runner. Unwilling to lay aside present pleasures, he has given in to temptations to run outside his prescribed lane. His life is filled with short cuts and dead-ends. He has few convictions and takes no costly stands in life. He just blends in with the pack!

The Callous Runner. This is a veteran runner who's become a cynic or is sarcastically critical of people. Scared by the puzzling, unfair circumstances of life, he seldom sees God in his everyday circumstances. Preoccupied with his injuries, his heart contains layers of thick, tough tissue made of bitterness, envy, or apathy.

The Committed Runner. Here's one who knows where the finish line is and who is determined to win. "In training" at all times, he knows that victory will never be achieved by the fainthearted. He has decided to run to win.

The Danger of Disqualification

If you're in the race and running, don't let anyone hinder you from running well. But beware, lest you are disqualified. Look back at Paul's warning at the end of the passage.

What does Paul mean when he says, "lest I myself should be disqualified"? Well, for one, he is not talking about losing his salvation. The Bible doesn't teach that we can be "unborn" from the family of God. I don't think it's a matter of just one mistake he's speaking of, but rather a repeated rejection of God's leading in life—willful, deliberate disobedience.

Look around at the human debris of those who have been disqualified from their ministry and usefulness to God. Do you know a Christian leader who is no longer in the race? A solid Christian layman or woman who once walked with Christ but no longer does? The landscape surrounding my life is littered with the lives of those who are sidelined. Casualties. I don't condemn those who fail, for my humanity is cut from the same bolt of human cloth. But they have become examples, living exhibits, warning me that I too could be disqualified and declared "no longer usable" by God.

Could you be disqualified? Absolutely. Could I? You bet!

Let me ask you a very important question: Is there anything in your life right now that could disqualify you? Something you're trying to hide? Something you're keeping from God? Don't mess around with sin. Don't play games with evil. It's deadly stuff.

Running to Win

So how do you run to win? Here are the apostle Paul's rules for the race:

1. *Self-control.* Paul speaks of competition runners who "exercise self-control in all things." The discipline of our desires is the backbone of our character. Know what tempts you and avoid it. Augustine, the great Christian philosopher, lived a licentious life before his conversion. One day, shortly after becoming a believer, Augustine encountered a young woman with whom he had sinned. Augustine turned immediately and began running away as the woman cried out, "Augustine! Augustine! It is I! It is I!" But Augustine just kept running, and yelled back over his shoulder, "It isn't I! It isn't I! It isn't I!"

2. *Careful aim or direction.* Paul says a runner intending to

win must know where he is going. The finish line for the Christian is the Person of Jesus Christ. Keep your eyes on Him. Grow in your love for Him. Be pleasing to Him. One of the reasons we indulge ourselves as spectators and have so little desire to give up our rights for the race before us is that we have lost our focus on the glory of God. When God is reduced in stature we begin to loose all desire to run to win. Don't lose focus.

3. *Sacrifice.* The Christian life will cost you your life. You and I must deny our rights and die to ourselves. Any prize, any relationship, anything of value *costs.* You may find that working through a problem in a relationship is harder than walking out. But walking out may result in God being through with you.

Going For It!

When Max and his running partner were about half way through their race up the slopes of Mount Whitney, they realized they could set a new American record. Together they decided to go for it. A friend who followed them the entire way said of them, "You could see the pain in their eyes. They looked like corpses after forty miles of continuous running . . . But at the finish there were tears in our eyes. It was something to be proud of." The pain was worth it! And for you and me, *the pain of living for Christ is worth it!*

I've decided not to turn my Reeboks in early. By God's grace I'll wear them out!

How about you: Are you going for it?

34.

Seeing
the Invisible

Planting the seed of meaningful achievement.

Jonathan Swift wrote in 1699, "Vision is the art of seeing the invisible."

It was a vision to reach the unreached that sent Dr. John Geddie to the people at Aneityum. Today a stone tablet bears testimony of Geddie's vision for these unreached people and his faithfulness for twenty-four years of service. Its inscription is a challenge to us today:

> When he landed in 1848, there were no Christians.
> When he left in 1872, there were no heathen.[1]

Geddie had a vision, a dream, and he gave his life to the fulfillment of it. Just one man. One man whose life bore the mark of the eternal invading the temporal.

But not all people look at the future with such expectancy. Maybe you know someone who lacks vision. If so, that person has some famous company. I came across an advertisement that contained the following group of quotations that illustrate that the seemingly unthinkable is not impossible:

> "Everything that can be invented has been invented."
> Charles H. Duell
> Director, U.S. Patent Office — 1899

> "Who the #$* wants to hear actors talk?"
> Harry M. Warner
> Warner Brothers Pictures — 1927

> "Heavier than air flying machines are impossible."
> Lord Kelvin
> President, Royal Society — 1895

> "Babe Ruth made a big mistake when he gave up pitching."
> Tris Speaker
> Baseball player and record holder — 1921

Not exactly the kind of "vision" referred to by Jonathan Swift and lived out by Dr. John Geddie, are they? I have to wonder what visions and dreams lie buried, forgotten, and dismissed today.

We remember Martin Luther King's dream. But when was the last time you had one? A dream of true renaissance? A dream of change, of radical departure from the norm?

If we as Christians have a direct relationship with the Creator of heaven and earth (and we do), then doesn't it stand to reason that we should be the most innovative and creative people on earth?

Do you believe God is through with creating? Or do you believe God has an eternal purpose, a destiny for your life? For your mate? Your children? Your grandchildren? Do you believe

God can give you a vision for your world that will captivate you for the rest of your life?

Questions for all of us are: "Do I really want to know the Creator's vision for my life?" "Do I want it to become a reality?" "Am I willing to follow Him at all costs?"

Listen carefully to the words of Paul: "For we are His workmanship, created in Christ Jesus for good works, which God prepared beforehand, that we should walk in them" (Ephesians 2:10).

The Christian life is not just fire insurance. It is an opportunity to walk daily within the will of God. It is the opportunity to lay up eternal treasures in heaven. It is the opportunity to lead others into Christ's kingdom.

What Do You Dream About?

When you dream, do you dream about things of God — the truly permanent things — or the things of the world, the truly perishable things? For what are you uniquely burdened? What injustice causes you to pound the table and weep?

A godly vision for your life will be characterized by incensed indignation toward the status quo. It will rock boats. Remember, they crucified our Savior because He shook up the system. A godly vision will be fueled by "what could be" and "what should be." It is an earnest quest for God's alternative.

Does your family have a vision that will affect the present and the eternal? Or are you just drifting with the flow of things?

Are you helping your children believe they have a destiny for their life? Are you adding fuel to their dreams and visions, or are you throwing water on them? Are you helping them see the eternal in the midst of time?

Do you want your family to follow you? Remember, it's hard to follow an insignificant person with trivial goals.

One of the major reasons for the identity crisis today in our culture is that we have lost a sense of destiny. There is no calling. No real mission. The feeling pervades that "nothing is truly worthy of my life."

Gaining Vision

So how do I acquire a sense of mission? How do I gain a vision for my life and family?

First, *pray*. Ask God to so burden your heart with someone or something that you can't let go. By the way, this process may take several months. Sometimes I think God wants to see if we're really serious about the whole thing!

Second, *look back over the tapestry of your life*. Are there any threads that continue to show up repeatedly? God may have been preparing you for just this moment, for just this set of circumstances, and for just this certain issue.

Third, *begin to talk about your idea with a few friends,* starting with your mate and family. Be careful here. Sometimes the Christian community can be intimidated and threatened with a burden from the Lord. It's sort of guilt-producing to listen to another's vision when you don't have one of your own!

Fourth, *count the costs (Luke 14) and then do something about it*. And if you start it, finish it.

Fifth, *be warned: Once God has directed, it is in our best interest to obey*. Remember Jonah?

One final note: In dreaming of the future, don't overlook the needs of the present. Recently I have asked many of our friends this question: *"If you could accomplish only one thing this year, what would it be?"*

Why not write your answer to that question on two 3x5 cards. Give one to your mate or a close friend who will hold you accountable, and then put the other on your calendar. Every month. Then begin to pencil into your schedule what you will need to do in order to meet that objective.

By the way, I don't know where Aneityum is, either. But I'll bet the people who live there know who Dr. John Geddie is.

May you follow Christ in being a dreamer and gaining vision for your life and your family.

1. Oswald Sanders, *Spiritual Leadership* (Chicago: Moody Press, 1967).

35.
Believing Is Seeing

Hope is no companion of doubt.

*H*ave you ever noticed how creative some businesses are at communicating their service or product through a catchy name or slogan?

The slogan of Johnson's Flower and Garden Center in Washington, D.C., is "Our Business is Blooming!" Our garbage company has one of my favorites: "We guarantee satisfaction or double your garbage back!"

American Way magazine recently had a story on others who get their message across in their name, like a car rental agency in

New York named "Chariots for Hire"; there's the "Auto Orphanage" in Sacramento; "Franks for the Memory," a hot dog stand on the West Coast. "The Recovery Room," a Salt Lake City upholstery shop; and "Shampooches," a self-service dog wash in (where else but) California!

Beauty shops seem to be the innovative leaders in this trend: "The Clip Joint," "Hair Port," "Hair It Is," "The Mane Event," "The Great Hair After," "The Gang's All Hair," "Take It From The Top," and my favorite, "We Curl Up and Dye!"

Sometimes the message in these names and slogans can really cause us to stop and think, like the antique store named "The Den of Antiquity" in Las Vegas.

But one grabbed my attention the other day. A Christian optometrist named his practice, "Seeing is Believing." When I saw that one, my mind raced back eighteen years to when I graduated from junior college.

A Turning Point

I was a normal twenty-year-old in the midst of the tumultuous days of the late sixties. I had no purpose. My life was chock-full of compromise, mediocrity, doubt, perplexing questions I couldn't answer, and frequent despair.

Everything I had touched for the past year had turned to gold—grades, girls, and college athletics. You would have thought I had everything, but I had lost my faith. I guess you would have called me a "backsliding Christian." I felt I had to *see it to believe it*. I was a twentieth-century doubting Thomas.

Precariously balanced with one foot on the banana peel of doubt and the other foot in the world, I began to honestly seek what God had to say about life—especially my life.

Throughout my quest one question haunted me: *"Must I really see it to believe it?"*

My slippery spiritual descent was halted in the fall of 1968 with the help of a number of people whom God brought across my path. Through those people, God loved me out of my spiraling unbelief.

The Agony of Questions

One of them was an evangelist named Tom Skinner. Tom shared a quote with me that I have shared with thousands:

> I spent a long time trying to come to grips with my doubts, when suddenly I realized I had better come to grips with what I believe. I have since moved from the agony of questions that I cannot answer, to the reality of answers that I cannot escape . . . and it's a great relief.

You see, my life was riddled with questions I couldn't answer:

- Is the Bible really God's Word?
- Why does God allow suffering?
- Where did evil come from?
- Will the heathen in foreign countries who have never heard about Jesus Christ really go to hell?
- Is Jesus Christ really Who He claims to be—God?
- If Christianity is a hoax, what is the purpose to life?

Ultimately, I doubted God's existence.

Hope is no companion of doubt.

It was as though I were saying, "Don't bother me with the truth. I'm having far too much fun being critical and grappling over issues that have confounded the philosophers for centuries." As someone once said, I was trying to unscrew the inscrutable.

The Obvious Truths

I began to see that struggling over questions that can't be answered on this side of heaven's gate was a waste of my life. This thought began to dawn upon me: *Why spend life questioning every minute detail of the Christian faith when there are so many obvious truths that can't be ignored?*

So I began to focus on what I knew to be true. I knew the resurrection was true. If Christ is still in the tomb then Christianity has little more to offer me than other world religions. But it is an irrefutable fact of history—*Christ is risen.*

I knew the Bible to be true. I still have plenty of unanswered questions about it, but those questions are only "featherweights" compared to the "heavyweight" truths about this supernatural book.

Its sixty-six different books were written by more than twenty different authors, separated by as much as 1600 years, through different cultures and in three different languages. We have more evidence that the Bible we have today is what was written originally than any other historical document of its age.

Science and archaeology continue to prove (rather than disprove) the Bible's historical accuracy. And its central theme remains clear: God loves mankind and wants to redeem men and women to Himself.

It tells us how to live. It gives us hope in the face of death. And it contains the best set of blueprints for building a home (a marriage and family) that I've ever seen.

One additional truth also helped me assassinate my doubts: I knew that the risen Lord Jesus Christ *lives* in me. He came to change my life. I found that Christianity is not boring, but a relationship with God.

Focus on the Facts

As I focused on the facts of Christianity I began to see the scales of faith tip toward belief. I began to base my life on what I knew to be true.

And for eighteen years now I've attempted to live my life on what I know to be true. What have been the results?

- A life that is an adventure. Walking with God is electrifying.

- A lasting sense of destiny and significance that isn't man-made or fake.
- The privilege of being used by God for eternal purposes.
- His Holy Spirit empowers me to deny my selfishness and enables me to love people (some of whom I don't even like).
- A sense of peace, well-being, and contentment that can only come when I obey Him.

Maybe for a Christian optometrist the phrase "Seeing Is Believing" is a good one, but if you wait to believe until you see all your doubts and questions answered, you'll be waiting for the rest of your life.

"For we walk by faith and not by sight" (2 Corinthians 5:7).

36.
Lion's
Breath

Have you ventured near the lions lately?

I've been smelling lion's breath recently, and have nearly gagged at its odious smell.

Where have I been? On a lion country safari? In Kenya? Sudan? South Africa? At the zoo? Or did our children get a pet lion?

No. None of these.

Let's just say I've been in lion country.

Pastor, author and lecturer A. W. Tozer made numerous

visits there. In fact, he may have lived in lion country. After a particularly difficult time in his ministry, Tozer noted the following: "But I will tell you something—it is a delightful thing when you know that you are close enough to the adversary that you can hear him roar! Too many Christians never get into 'lion country' at all!"

After pondering Tozer's observation, I've concluded that we not only *should,* but absolutely *must* charge off into lion country. I've learned that spiritual conflict means we're about to do something worthwhile, that will last for eternity.

What about you? Have you taken a spiritual safari into lion country? Do you know where it is?

Enemy Territory

"Lion country" is territory controlled by the devil. It is the daily domain of the ruler of this world. The apostle John comments on its location: "We know that we are of God and the whole world is in the power of the evil one" (1 John 5:19).

Because God has given Satan permission to rule on earth, a struggle for power and dominion has resulted. Yet many Christians are unaware that enemy territory even exists. Peter warns, "Be of sober spirit, be on the alert. Your adversary, the devil, prowls about like a roaring lion, seeking someone to devour" (1 Peter 5:8).

Lions in Africa prey on weak, unsuspecting animals and those straggling behind the protection of the head of the pack. Likewise, the devil prowls about trying to deceive (devour) those with weak convictions and naive beliefs. Christians who refuse to submit to the accountability of other believers in the local church find themselves isolated and defenseless, delicious prey for the crafty deceptor.

How does a lion devour its prey? One bite at a time. I wonder at times if twentieth-century Christians have been anesthetized by prosperity and busy schedules while the enemy chews off three-quarters of their legs!

Instead of falling prey, Christians must be aggressive soldiers recapturing the land for Christ. The goal of our battle is to confine the enemy to limited spheres of influence, just as the lions of Africa are limited to the confines of game preserves. When Christ returns, He will lock up the enemy forever (Revelation 20).

So why all the fuss about lion country?

Deceived Into Mediocrity

Far too many Christians are being fooled by the enemy. They have been deceived into thinking that run-of-the-mill Christianity is all there is.

Dabbling in spiritual things, they "play church." Jesus Christ may be a part of their lives, but He isn't their *life*.

I know, because I've been there. For more than fourteen years I was the prey of the enemy. I thought I knew what was best for me. I ran the show. I wanted God only as my emergency Savior, when I was in a crisis and needed Him.

Armed with the gospel, the greatest truth the world has ever heard, we fearfully retreat to our spiritual bunkers and wait for an unsaved world to come to us. Instead of invading, we disengage and play it safe.

But there's more to Christianity than that.

Successful invaders are risk-takers. Men and women of faith and action. The victory will go to those who are willing to move their faith the eighteen-inch distance from their head to their heart. Victory belongs to those who start the race and, with God's grace, finish it.

Many Christians, however, seem to prefer comfort to conflict.

I've been reading a book about Winston Churchill. Churchill believed the battlefield is the place where great issues are resolved. And I believe that the great issues of our day will never be decided when we sip lemonade in a hammock, but rather when well-equipped Christians invade lion country. Just as Churchill refused to negotiate until the adversary had capitulated, neither can we afford to give in to temptation or compromise.

Yes, lion country is a dangerous challenge to be taken seriously. The evil one hates God and is a serious enemy of our soul. We must arm ourselves for battle (Ephesians 6:10-20).

Heard the Roar of Lions Lately?

Get on with it! The greatest thrill in your life will come when you know you're encroaching on the enemy's territory.

As you do, remember these five tips from the Scripture:

1. Stand firm. We have God's assurance that we won't lose the war. You have absolutely nothing to be afraid of (Ephesians 6).

2. Let God's Word be your guide. And don't wait until you get eaten alive to start studying the Scriptures. Now is the time to prepare for battle (Ephesians 6).

3. Pray always and give thanks frequently. Praise is one of the most powerful weapons a Christian has in spiritual battle. Have you truly praised God for your battle? (1 Thessalonians 5:16-18).

4. Know that no temptation is to be taken lightly. Sin is deadly. Flee immorality. Tell the truth. Speak kindly one to another (2 Timothy 2).

5. Walk by faith, *not* by *feelings* and what you can see. God's Word and His promises are either 100 percent true or they are not true at all. Since His Word is true, your faith is the difference. Grab hold of His Word and step out (2 Corinthians 5:7).

C. T. Studd, the great missionary to China, understood the challenge well. He wrote, "Some people want to live within the sound of chapel bells, but I want to run a mission a yard from the gate of hell."

Do you want to be comfortable, or do you want to be Christlike? If you want to be like Christ, then you are sure to hear the footsteps of lions.

The battle has been tough for me recently, but I wouldn't trade being in lion country for any of the peace and comfort that depended on compromise.

What about you?

37.

The Illusion of Tomorrow

Life is but brief. Let's not put off today what can be done tomorrow. Tomorrow may never come.

I went to my next-door-neighbor's funeral today. He was forty-one years old. It was like other funerals, solemn and heavy with grief. Death had once again taken a life and left the living in a reflective daze evaluating their own lives.

The problem is that it sometimes takes something as weighty as death to get our attention. We live daily as though we are immortal, as though we will never have to face our own grave.

Procrastination—putting off until tomorrow the commitment that needs to be made today — seems to be as old as death it-self. We hope things will fall into place. It's interesting to me how we tend to procrastinate on some of the most important decisions and actions of our lives.

- Saying words of encouragement, appreciation, and love to our mate.
- Putting our arms around our children and hugging them (regardless of their age).
- Playing with our children.
- Writing that letter of appreciation to our parents for all their hard work and labor in raising us right.
- Settling accounts with God once and for all.
- Committing our lives fully to Christ as Lord and Savior.
- Living for eternity instead of for the moment.

Procrastination seems to lull its victims to sleep, giving them a false sense of security. It moves us steadily, slowly, methodical-ly toward living lives of destruction. Its companions are mediocrity, compromise, laziness, lies, broken vows and promises, escapism, fantasizing, and daydreaming.

Solomon knew about procrastination. In his concluding chap-ter of Ecclesiastes, he writes with a piercing pen, "Remember God in the days of your youth." He places priority on remembering God not on our deathbed, nor in our middle age, but in our *youth*. Solomon urges us to add together, like pearls being strung, one day after another of walking with God. This results in a life that honors God rather than self. We stop going our own way and, instead, go God's way.

The Earlier, The Better

Reflecting on this passage and my neighbor's death, I am struck with how important it is to establish good habits early in our life. We must make those commitments to Christ and begin to follow them up. Young Christians who know and trust Christ and build a track record of walking with Him, grow up to become dynamic adults who remember God in their later years.

Instead of saying, "Why do it today when I can put it off until tomorrow, or next week, or next year," Solomon says, "Don't put it off any longer. Stop. Pray. Reflect. Think. Listen to God. Then actually choose to do it now." First we make our decisions, and then our decisions make us. Many people don't fail in their decisions; they fail because they never decide.

Procrastination tells God that He's a liar about priorities; He really doesn't know what life is all about. Procrastination makes a selfish and compromising statement. It asserts that we know best about today. Who cares about the Grim Reaper? Or the consequences for our wrong choices? Or, least of all, the Judgment?

Solomon also warns us to fear God. He summarizes the entire book by saying, "Remember God. Fear God." He's saying don't just remember God on Sundays, but revere God daily. Hold Him in awe. Practice His presence moment by moment. That will keep us from spiritual amnesia and procrastination.

Accountable to God

Procrastinators would do well with a good dose of the fear of the Lord in their veins. It might help them realize that they will ultimately stand accountable before God for the decisions they make today. We are not nearly as powerful as we think we are.

Finally, Solomon says, "Obey God." When all is said and done, remembering God and fearing God must ultimately work its way into our lifestyle in the form of obedience. Obedience to God's laws, His Word, His commands. Obedience to God's value system of life.

Chuck Swindoll has said, "It is never too late to start doing what is right." The procrastinator will always talk himself out of that one.

My next-door neighbor was a fine man. His friends spoke highly of him. However, on a morning in December, he arose as he had done every other morning, and went to the hospital to make his rounds as an orthopedic surgeon. He was one of the finest surgeons in the city, I am told, specializing in repairing broken hands.

After making his rounds and before going to his office, he stopped at the cleaners to pick up his laundry. As he stood at the counter, a woman (who recently had been raped) walked in, carrying her purse which contained a loaded gun. She accidentally dropped the purse on the floor. The gun discharged, and the bullet hit my neighbor in the head. He died eight hours later. The Lord had called my neighbor home for *his* day of accounting.

Have you been putting something off that you need to do?

God never procrastinates.

Are you ready?

38.

Dare
to Risk

Planting the seed of faith.

I am a daredevil, a risk taker. No, not the kind who goes hang-
gliding, shark-hunting, or white-water rafting on the Colorado
River at flood stage. Some of those things border on lunacy *for me*.
But I like adventure, trying something new with just enough risk
to make it exciting.

Last August I did something that causes me to tremble and
tighten my muscles even now as I think about it. My boss put
together a two-day stress camping adventure forty miles south of
Yosemite Valley in the central Sierra range in California for
several of the leaders of Campus Crusade for Christ. The purpose

was to create unity among the leadership. It did that and more.

The first night we slept under the shimmering stars. The evening air was cool and brisk. After a good night's sleep, steaming coffee and hot chocolate were big winners that chilly morning. Then we set out for our first day's challenge — mountain climbing.

Words and phrases like "rope up," "Belay ready," "rappelling," and "sewing machine leg" had new meaning. Five of us attacked a "little" thirty-foot mountain face while ten others held our lifeline (the rope) in case we slipped or fell.

As I sought indentations in that mountain for footing, my legs trembled so badly that they bounced up and down like a needle in a sewing machine — sewing machine leg! Sewing machine leg is humbling and annoying when you are trying to be a macho mountain man. Real men don't get sewing machine leg. Humiliation visited me quickly that day.

Each of us came to the conclusion — several times — that there was no way the rock could be climbed. To keep climbing, we had to mentally decide to take a risk. *Will that little ledge over there hold me?* The rope I was securely fastened to gave the ultimate bit of security needed to take the chance. I found that in most cases physical limitations were not my enemy. My mind caused me the real trouble, wanting to play it safe or to know the outcome for sure. Fear and faith took on new meanings.

Hanging On

I must admit it was humbling to see my boss scamper up that mountain like a squirrel. Others of us "hung around" a long time, bloodying our knuckles, knees and elbows before achieving our objective. No one quit. Deep inside, several of us wanted to quit, but among grown men the peer pressure was too great!

Supper was made from a bunch of dried stuff cooked in water. It tasted like oatmeal that had been run over several times by a city bus! That night sleep came early for most of us. The moonlight beamed brilliantly. From the valley where we camped, we could look up 1500 feet to the moonlit mountain where we would rappel the next day.

When morning came we wolfed down cereal and coffee. The packs on our backs were lighter. There was a lot of nervous laughter among these "experienced" mountaineers. Our professional guides (three of them) assured us that five thousand people had rappelled off that mountain and not a single one had ever received substantial injuries. The word "substantial" bothered me. Each of us was thinking, *I could be the first to die.*

Getting to the top of the rock dome was no easy task. I bloodied my left hand and was hit with another case of sewing machine leg before I scrambled to the top, 8500 feet high. You could see for miles up there. The sky was deep blue. The sun threatened to cook our noses.

We numbered off. I was number twelve out of fourteen, which meant I had about two and a half hours to think about sliding down a rope over the edge of a cliff to a ledge 175 feet below. Sometimes thinking is dangerous.

Real Men Don't Cry

Eleven men all acted like real men as they backed off the edge with two ropes securing them to the mountain. Real men don't cry, even though they feel like it, in front of their peers when rappelling off the top of a mountain.

Finally, it was my turn. With cold, sweaty palms, I stood to fasten my rope on my belt. Below me the mountain sloped at a 45-degree angle for five feet. At that point there was a lip to go over before dropping 175 feet to the ledge below. I didn't look back. I just leaned back on that rope, trusting, believing and hoping it would hold me.

At the edge of the lip I had to lean back almost horizontally. All those nightmares I've had of falling flashed through my mind.

This is it, I thought. *This is the way I'm going to die. At least it will be over quickly. No chance of dying by degrees here. One quick flight, a thud, and an oily spot!*

The rope held, and in a few seconds I found that I was dangling there with the valley floor 1500 feet below to my left. I glided safely down the rope for about thirty seconds to the ledge below. The risk had been worth it. I felt like kissing the ground, but real men don't do that either. Unhooking my ropes, I looked up at the mountain and thought, *I really can't believe I did that.*

The ride to the airport was filled with relief, laughter, and a unity that was indescribable. Fourteen men had done something that few ever do (or want to do). We *were* associated in ministry. *Now* we were a team of comrades for the Kingdom.

Ready to Move Mountains

Risk is inevitable if we are to climb mountains and accomplish great things for the Kingdom of God. Your mind may say, *Play it safe,* but the Scriptures tell us to believe before we see.

I also learned that Jesus is my Rock, the rock of my salvation. Those ropes were bolted in six places to that immovable mountain before we dangled our way to the bottom. Likewise, Christ our Rock is immovable. The Rock is secure in the storm. The Rock is our refuge, our strength, our safety. He is unshakable.

What then is the real need among Christians today? The real need is not safety, security, or a fat savings account. It is not better facilities, better programs, flashier television shows, a celebrity's testimony, more people in the ministry, or an open door for the gospel in a closed country. Those are all needs. But what is the real need?

Dawson Trotman, founder of the Navigators, was asked about the need of the hour. He replied, "The need of the hour is an army of soldiers dedicated to Jesus Christ *who believe* that He is God, that He can fulfill every promise He ever made, and that nothing is too hard for Him. This is the only way we can accomplish what is on God's heart, getting the gospel to every creature."

The real need is for risk-takers—those who dare to lean out over the cliff's edge on the promises of His word. Jesus called them *disciples.*

Depending on the Rock?

I can assure you I'm a novice, but if I keep going out over the edge, sooner or later I'm going to become a veteran in the faith.

A few questions flash through my mind:

- What are you risking for Christ?
- What dreams should you be attempting for the Kingdom?
- What would you do if you knew you could not fail?
- Is your goal safety or is it the work of the Kingdom?
- Are you controlled by fear or by faith?

Stepping out in faith doesn't have to be knee-jarring, heart-pounding, great, or spectacular. For some it may mean volunteering to teach a Sunday school class or increasing your giving. But for others the hazards may be more costly, such as witnessing to a boss or a neighbor. The risk includes the exposure that comes from attempting something only Jesus Christ can pull off in and through you.

Venture out! Don't play it safe. Life is too short. Remember Helen Keller's words: "Life is either a daring adventure or nothing." Find your true safety in Christ and go for it!

"He fills me with strength and protects me wherever I go. He gives me the surefootedness of a mountain goat upon the crags. He leads me safely along the top of the cliffs . . . You have given me your salvation as my shield. Your right hand, O Lord, supports me; your gentleness has made me great. You have made wide steps beneath my feet so that I need never slip" (Psalm 18:32-36).

What are you risking for Christ?

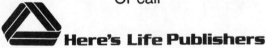

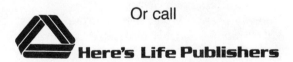

Resources for Your Marriage and Family

Dennis Rainey is national director of the Family Ministry, which provides several helpful resources to help you strengthen your marriage and family.

If you would like to receive information on an upcoming Family Life Conference in your area, or on the *Homebuilders Film Series* (a six-part series derived from the Family Life Conferences), please complete the response coupon below.

The Family Ministry has also developed the *Homebuilders Couples Series* — a small-group Bible study designed to provide positive guidance to husbands and wives based on biblical, workable principles. Check below to receive information on this study.

Dennis publishes a monthly newsletter, *My Soapbox,* which covers a variety of topics on the home, the family, and the Christian life. A one-year subscription is $15.

Please return the coupon to: FAMILY MINISTRY
P.O. Box 23840
Little Rock, AR 72211

TELL ME MORE!

I am interested in the following (please check):

_____ Family Life Conference brochure

_____ *Homebuilders Film Series*

_____ *Homebuilders Couples Series* (group Bible studies)

_____ *My Soapbox* (monthly newsletter, enclose $15)

Name _____

Address_____

City _____ State _____Zip _____